Lacunae

I0192845

Mind the Gaps

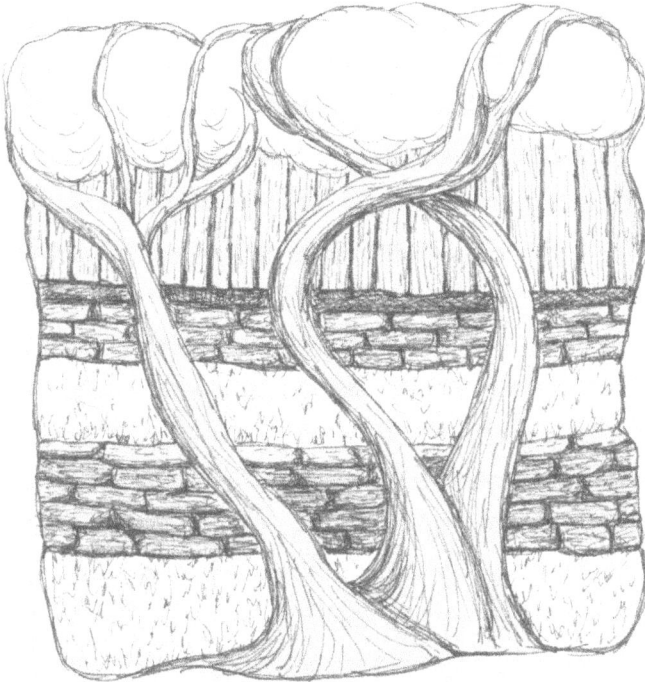

Lacunae are gaps, hiatuses, absences,
unfilled spaces or intervals, voids,
vacancies, missing portions,
in a book or manuscript, in art or music,
lapses of memory, hollow cavities, pits,
small openings, small blank spaces,
spaces visible between cells,
allowing the free passage of light.

Linda Varsell Smith

Filling Formatting and Illustration Gaps
Cover Art: "Bohemian Sunset"
Back Cover Art: "Fat"
Maureen Frank — TheMandalaLady.com

Filling Support Gaps
My poetry critique groups,
friends and family

Filling Publishing Gaps
ISBN: 978-0-9888554-9-6
© Copyright 2018 by Rainbow Communications

Rainbow Communications
471 NW Hemlock Ave.
Corvallis, OR 97330

varsell4@comcast.net

Filling the Gaps About Linda Varsell Smith

Linda was born in New Britain, Connecticut in 1940.
She graduated from Central Connecticut University in
Elementary Education and MS in Educational Psychology at
University of Arizona. With husband Court she raised two sons
and a daughter in Oregon. Linda taught elementary grades as
well as community college: creative writing, children's
literature, Life story as well as Literary Publication which
produced The Eloquent Umbrella magazine. For over thirty
years she was an editor at Calyx Books. She wrote series of
fantasy novels as well as poetry books. Linda was president of
the Oregon Poetry Association and is currently president of
Portland PEN Women. She belongs to Write the Wrongs to
Rights Huddle, plays competitive and cooperative Scrabble,
enjoys craft fairs, plays, dance, gymnastics, art and several
writing groups, gives poetry workshops and readings collects
miniatures of Swedish folk art and seasonal creatures–
thousands of angels, lives in a mini-museum.

Table of Contents

There is a gap between the mind and the world,
and (as far as anybody knows)
you need to posit internal representations
if you are to have a hope of getting it across.
Mind the gap. You'll regret it if you don't.

Jerry A. Fodor

Filling Gaps with Chi

Filling the Gaps..2
Mine the Gaps...3
The Entangling Spider..4
Diminishing Harvests...5
Mixed Messages...6
Fall Has Fallen...7
Thinking Like Da Vinci...8
The Fallen..10
Surround Sound...11
In Just October..12
Land of the Elderberries...14
Indigenous People Day...15
Full Moon in Aries...18
A Clean Slate...20
Deep Breathing..22
Shadowing...23
Seeing Red...24
Backyard in Autumn...25
Preparing for Rain..26
Autumnal Appraisal...27
Conjuring Witches...28
Halloween Haunts..29
Exiting October..30
Mutually Blue..31
Full Moon in Taurus...32
Downcast...33
Considering Change...35
Fairy Rings..36

Plucking the Fairy's Eyebrow...38
Noticing...40
Between Storms...41
The World Did Not End..43
Bluetiful..44
Inner Peace..45
Under Turbulent Clouds...47
A Real Rain..48
Nap-Zapper...49
The Angel Weathervane..50
Tootsie Toots Her Horn...51
The Silence Breakers...52
I Stand At the Window..54

Mining Creative Gaps

Seasonal Characters..56
The Witch Bitches About Gretel and Hansel....................................57
Attracting Bigfoot...59
High Tech Holidays...60
Santa's Lighting Agency..61
Santa's Delivery System..62
Scribes..63
Pen-Dancer...64
Dissecting Poetry and Science..65
Revising Fibs..66
The Omnificent English Dictionary in Limerick Form...........................67
Emoji..68
Instagram Poets..70
Twitter..71
Magical Realism..72
Images of Moleclues..73

Finding Spiritual Gaps

Experiencing the Gap...76
The Space Between Breaths..78
Blind Spots..80
Finding Meaning in an Existential Vacuum.....................................81
My Body..82

Homo Universalis..83
In the Wings...84
Cosmic Intermediaries..85
Message from Jayne..86
The Elders Return.. 87
Mindfulness Meditation...89
The Happy Ending..90
Cosmic To-Do List...91
Animation... 92
Inner Light.. 93
Finding Bliss... 94
Helping Hands... 95

Exposing Personal Gaps

A Feather... 98
My Found Feather... 100
Decorating My Home..101
Untidy..102
Playing Golf with Phlebotomists....................................103
Becoming a Dalmatian.. 104
Chocolate Therapy..105
Changing the Bed... 106
Sleepy in Corvallis..108
The Risers..109
Cosmic Life Process...110
On a Dream Cruise.. 111
Night Travel...112
Excursion at Safeway... 113
Not P. C. With P.J.'s.. 114
The Demise of My Pajamas..116
Searching for Pajamas...117
Senior Exercise Class...118
Falling on the Winter Solstice..119
New Steps in Fitness..120
Tale of the Tri-Color Hair..121
Tri-Color Hair #2...123
Tri-Color Hair #3...124
Truly Blue...125
Greetings for Now...126

Geek E-mail.. 127
What Have You Learned This Year? 128
Clowns.. 129
When Is Enough, Enough...130
New Year's Resolutions...131

Pondering Gaps in Origins

On My Mind.. 134
Hopefully We Are Not Alone....................................135
Symbols..136
Mass Extinctions...137
Tardigrades: Sole Survivors? 139
Hidden Knowledge... 140
Creating Better Human Beings................................142
Becoming Superhuman...143
Digging Up Fossils... 144
Interpreting the Past..145
Finding Ancient Homo Sapiens...............................146
Neanderthals Grew Slowly...Like Homo Sapiens...........147
Doom of Neanderthals.. 148
Pondering the Annunaki...149
Remnants... 150

Exploring Cosmic Gaps

Cosmic Communication... 152
Cosmic Complaint Bureau...153
Starselves.. 155
Pleiades Mythology..156
Cosmic Dances...159
Stargazer... 160
Oumuamua: "Messenger From Afar Arriving First"...................161
Celestial Tanka String.. 162
Jupiter Moves in with Scorpio.................................. 163
Mysterious Saturn Rings... 165
Losing Cassini: September 15, 2017......................... 167
Saturn's Moons.. 168
Moon Tunnel...169
Haumea: The Ringed Dwarf Planet.........................170

Ross 128-B and Beyond..171
Oldest, Farthest Black Hole...172
I Wonder Why...176

Gleaning Global Gaps

Disconnected? 177
Shifting Through Dimensions.......................................178
The Week that Was...179
Ecological Roulette...180
Plastics Shall Inherit the Earth....................................181
Trashing Henderson Island..183
Fatbergs...184
Tunneling...185
Invading the Doomsday Vault......................................186
International Day of Peace..187
Flaming Hell..188
Searching for Yonies...189
Smog..190
Warning to Humanity...191
2018 is an 11 Year...192

Protesting Unfulfilled Gaps

Raise Your Words and Voice..194
Language of Resistance...195
Sign For The TImes...196
Slacktivism..197
The Good Samaritans..198
Standing Up for Each Other..199
Ron Wyden Town Hall..200
Dealing With the News...201
A Tiki Torch in Charlottesville......................................202
Fading Moral Values..204
A New Story...205
Cyber Attacks...207
Fearless Girl...208
Pink Balloons...209
Pro-Femina..210
The Dirt on Men...212

#ResistMarch June 11, 2017...213
Hateful Shadows...214
Trump is "Sad"...215
Another Bloody Mess...216
Trumpifiring..217
Swollen Minds..218
Whacks for July 4th Holiday 2017....................................220
Derailed..223
Searching for Truths..224
First Supermoon This Year...225
Bridging the Gaps...228

Lacunae of Light

Filling Gaps With Light..229
Sources of Light...230
If Life is But a Dream...231
Children of the Earth Monument......................................232
Start Each Day...233
Walk-Kissers...234
Light Showers...235
To Be or Not To Be..236
The Character Gap...237
Time's Up...239
Acknowledgments...241

Filling Gaps with Chi

*What's the difference between people who see and seek gaps
and those that see and seek bridges? The first stops
and stays on the side. The second crosses and reaches
a new world...As soon as your mind identifies the bridge,
the gap is gone... you just had to see it. But everything
is first created in your mind and then in the world.
The bridge is there. See it. Cross it.*

Richie Norton

Filling the Gaps

John Ashberry stood out for his audacity and for his wordplay, for his modernist shifts between high oratory and everyday chatter, for his humor and wisdom and dazzling runs of illusions and sense impressions... His poems emphasize verbal surprise and delight, not the ways that linguistic patterns restrict us.
        Hillel Italie

This serotinal, sunny, smoky morning,
I sit in the backyard for my daily dose of chi
with a different intention.

The original purpose of connecting earth
and cosmic chi was to energize healing.
I want to energize creativity as well.

When I contemplate, I want to focus on
what gaps in my curiosity and understanding
I should explore in poetry, opening boundaries.

This concept begins this new, open-ended book.
Mirabilia is ready for printing proof this week.
Spiral Hands awaits editing and illustration.

Lacunae could have similar intents as Ashberry's,
but I relish word-play experiments with forms--
filling gaps of rhythm, rhyme and content.

Surrounded by a kaleidoscope of images:
garbage trunk dumps waste, plane poops contrail,
windfall apples plop polka-dots on lawn...

Lots of unloading. I want to upload ideas
to plug the lacunae in my knowledge,
to dance down flexible lines.

A pesky wasp threatens to sting--circles.
    Take the hint and leave!
        Go inside to probe and play!

Clear the air.
    Root and wing.
                Breathe deeply.

Mine the Gaps

The back fence reveals a missing slat,
a gap allowing an incomplete view
of the other side of the boundary.

Supported, like upper and lower braced teeth
with a removed tooth, there is a gap,
an unbalance, a place to probe.

I like to explore the gaps in unknowing,
wondering if I can fill these openings
with understanding and insight.

I'm not an underground miner.
Not into digging dirt, revealing metals,
taking Gaia's guts for my glory.

I'm more an observer of gaps
pondering why they exist, why
they still invite exploration.

I'm a word-miner, searching for light
a flashlight in a cave, spotlight on land,
searchlight to the sky.

Behind the boards, the fence slices views
of a gold and white cat–head seen in open gap.
I await the cat to emerge glowing golden and whole.

The Entangling Spider

A spider sways on invisible thread--
(at least it appears so to these less acute eyes)
tethered to a filbert limb.

She sways seemingly independent
of the gentle breeze in jerky motions.
The wind chimes barely ting.

In a certain slant of light the spider
looks orangy like the smoky morning sun,
then shades to brown.

Just dangling there, floating, does she
plan to lasso prey? She risks disconnection
by buggy passerby or clueless human.

In a light-shift I see her intricate, finely
woven web with tiny orts. Possible meals?
Ash? Wind debris or dust?

She is about four feet from my chair.
Since I spied her widening operation,
I consider my movements carefully.

In her fluctuations, she becomes closer.
I ponder metaphors from world-wide web,
Spiderman, to webs of deception and illusion.

She has not ensnared another insect.
Wasps and bees hover over and on
the apple-dappled lawn.

My focus changes to hurricanes Harvey, Irma, monsoons,
the cancellation of DACA, threats from North Korea,
wildfires, heat waves and ineffectual governance.

Next incarnation I might consider being a spider
creating exquisite webs, floating like an angel.
But spiders construct snares.

Each of us a thread in the cosmic fabric?
An energetic signature, part of ALL?
Today Earth appears so fragile.

Diminishing Harvests

Almost October, I don a poofy jacket, carry
a blue pillow to warm and soften the black
metal seat where I absorb backyard chi.

The fruit and nut harvests are diminishing
or gone. Still, too many apples and pears
to eat or give away to humans or horses.

Framed between the fork of the hazelnut trunk
I see a golden pear on a branch and a windfall.
My husband plucks and plunks them in a bucket.

One pear was top-chopped. On the way
to throw it away, he found windfall apples–
one gnawed and one pecked. No wasps or bees.

Small dark birds (about four inches long)
with white stripes on the side of their heads, peck
at bark, ground, even the metal storage shed roof.

They make a squeaky sound, part of the squawk
in surrounding yards. Fewer birds recently–
especially with the demise of filberts. No butterflies.

Leaves curl and fall. Do their exercise crunches?
Cradle the air? Enjoy winging it with birds,
fairies and angels? Just a death spiral?

I miss the cherry tree we had to remove
due to borers. The cherry crop was poor.
We seeded grass on the mound, not a tree.

Cloud-dimmed sun splayed faded shade.
As the sun broke free of shroud, the shadows
darkened, only to disappear as sky grayed.

I witness the onslaught of autumn. Next will
be a lap blanket to warm my thoughts and body,
comfort for my sun-hugger heart, limbs and soul.

Mixed Messages

Summer and autumn seem to be in a tug of war.
After months of sizzling hot, a respite of rain and chill,
now back to days of dry, 80 degree heat to enter October.

I gather warm chi, chew an oatmeal raisin cookie
with scent of grilled chicken lunch on my hands.
The wasps stays with the chomped apple leftover.

My husband took down the side gate to keep out
deer, since we have few fruit left. So I have no idea
whether deer or raccoon might have provided the wasp snack.

Deer might be hiding in the woods since it is hunting
season, but they might find more safety in the suburbs
where they are less likely to get shot. A deer night-nibbler?

We gave away the last apple and pear bucket yesterday.
The rest, hanger-ons, are designated for domestic use.
I count two golden pears and four red apples buttoning the lawn.

The green hose graces the cherry tree's grave.
The black hose coils beside the black plastic
wheelbarrow Pisa-leaning against the green back wall.

Several white empty buckets surround one fruit-full
bucket. A few indecisive LBJs (little brown jobbers)
peck bark, beak-poke grass, flit branch to branch.

The apple tree bleeds some red fungus.
It sure looks deceptively like blood. Reddening
leaves appears as drops of blood.

A solo yellow butterfly flutters near the fence.
Since I had not seen one in a few days, I assumed
its season was over. Today's warmth postponed demise?

The feather I found is not a feather in my cap
for I have no headband on any of my hats--just
part of the global mixed messages I can't decipher.

Fall Has Fallen.

Fall has fallen. Rain and temperature fell.
No shadows on the lawn. No bugs or butterflies.
Not even a dandelion to mimic sun.

It is almost October. Oregon expects rain.
I forgot to cover my chi chair or take in pillow.
I have a soggy seat. Rain drips off shower curtain cover.

An apple plops to form a triangle.
Only small birds in branches.
Neighbors' yards have more bird chirps.

There is a lull in hurricanes. Relief
efforts in force in Texas, Florida, Puerto Rico
and the Caribbean, but access poor.

I check my watch to see if I have been outside
long enough to absorb chi from gray sky
and damp ground. A lollygagging loop today?

I lug the lumpy pillow inside,
cover the chair with the curtain.
My jacket never unzipped.

I throw the pillow in the drier
full of dry clothes. Two, yarn-wrapped,
tennis-type balls fluff and thump.

Fortunately, I am heading for a massage
with warm stones. I decide not to change
my wet pants. Body heat is on duty.

I ache. I am cold. Yesterday was warm
and sunny. But now the forecast is for
more days like this one. Fall has fallen.

Thinking Like Da Vinci

*History's most creative genius was not superhuman and following his methods
can bring great intellectual rewards to anyone. Be curious, observe attentively
and indulge fantasy.* Walter Issacson

Near noon on a gray-dampened day, I carry
my dry pillow to the backyard to connect with
wonder on my innernet, try to think like Leo.

I toss off the rain-covering on my chi chair and sit,
trying to draw creativity into my chi loop.
I zip my jacket to trap warmth, rev energy.

I am curious why fallen leaves wind-whirl in clusters,
leaving some more isolated and alone. Will-of-the-wind
repositions them for their next transition?

I study the unpicked-up, windfall apples' daily
re-designs, new constellations. Does unknown energy
thrusts guide landings or thrown randomly?

I observe the LBJs I thought were Little Brown Jobbers
peck at the bark of a nearby hazelnut tree. The head
has white stripes, orange belly, black back.

So they are Little Black Jobbers. The orange and black
combo are OSU Beavers colors. They fit in the local
university hype. The Stellar Jays more cosmic blue.

I fantasize a Trump-less, tweet-less world where
birds tweet and people communicate with competence
and social conscience. We need more Leonardos.

I have no problem believing everything has energy
and consciousness. Now, how to figure out access to higher
realms and channel it like creative geniuses have claimed.

Leo's human flaws do not detract from his insights, but I
don't believe humans have equal access. Cultures and cosmos
have prevented women from expressing and receiving creativity.

Or is it from source on cosmic level and other dimensions
discriminating against women receiving downloads
as well as other minority groups? Leo had extra perks?

Leo was considered "wildly imaginative, quirkily curious,
and willfully observant." Can less-endowed mortals
tap into and emulate his resources? Free will enough?

Vision without execution is hallucination, Issacson claims.
Leonardo's ability to blur the line between reality
and imagination was the key to his creativity.

He suggests we can try to cultivate these skills to put
imagination to productive use. Our lives will be the better
for it. Never outgrow the need to know why.

Be curious about everything. Check.
I'm always open to learning something new.
I try to understand the unknowable.

Observe attentively. Check.
When teaching writing, I advocate: pay attention.
Despite blurry vision, I try to see clearly, process patterns.

Indulge fantasy. Check.
I collect and imagine inanimate objects, wrote 12 fantasy novels.
I'm fascinated by multi-dimensionality, easy to imagine-elsewhere.

Like Leo I keep notebooks. Not as artistic or scientific,
but I record inquiries and insights. I do not aspire to be him.
I just want to glean all the wonder my consciousness can.

My experiments are not the level of Leo, but we are
all unique and can contribute our best to humanity,
to cosmic consciousness, Akashic records, living library.

My time is up for now thinking with Leo. I pull down
the shower curtain over chi chair and go inside
to plunk a few computer keys, network with nets.

The Fallen

Honor what you feel, not what you fear.   John Edward

Yesterday in just-October when I went into
the backyard to energize my chi, one apple
fell before me. Only a few diehards left on limbs.

Seeded grass covers more of the cherry
tree's grave. Lacy lichen, like tiny doilies,
applique white on the rain-greened lawn.

Wind-chimes jingle with the rhythm
of the chilly breeze and bird chirps.
Pillow on the chair kept the seat warm.

Today it is sunny, black shadows well-defined.
I layered for the cold. One raccoon-relished,
gouged apple on the moist grass.

Enough apples and leaves have fallen,
so deep pink peek-a-boos through the branches
from the back neighbor's tall reddening tree.

Smaller than LBJ birds camouflage with
shivering leaves. A lone stellar jay swishes
through without landing. No bugs. Few chimes.

The bad news of the day is the largest mass shooting
in Las Vegas at The Harvest Country Music Festival
at the Mandalay Bay. Still counting dead and injured.

Suddenly the backyard imagery turns dark.
The pinky leaves seem bloody, not blushing autumn.
The leaves–the fallen. The shadows–grief.

I can understand seasonal change,
natural transitions, even adapt to most unnatural
climate changes imposed by irresponsible people...

but when guns take away choice and free will
by actions of the shooter, violence causes fear,
damage and death, I can only grieve the fallen,

despair and get angry at the waste, dark deceitful
motives, the misguided beliefs and addled brains
that darkle light and love with hate. I pray for hope.

10

Surround Sound

As I sit absorbing chi, I am surrounded
by sounds which distract my contemplation--
plaintive meows of an unseen cat,

clanging wind-chimes in brisk breeze
also rustling leaves, some leaves wrestled
from reddening bushes and trees, fall.

Birds of various hues and sizes
squawk, chirp, coo, across fences.
Local and highway traffic coughs, chokes,

murmurs, rat-a-tat backfires like gunfire.
All the inside media repeats the conversation,
on gun control and tragedies like Las Vegas.

I am bombarded by sounds. My backyard is usually
relatively quiet. Usually I can tune out noises or they
are a temporary glitch, but today I attune.

I've come from exercise class and the caterwaul
of cat owners, discussion of Dancing With the Stars--
politics and religion are verboten, but not mass killings.

Like victims of natural disasters, victims of violence
will get their vigils, prayers, tributes to courageous
helpers of survivors left to rebuild shattered lives.

Endless calls for assistance, donations, speculation
what we can do to prevent catastrophes. Some problems
can be lessened by banning and planning, Go Fund Me pleas.

How many shootings have to happen to institute
gun control? Bought Congressmen will not buck
the gun lobby. Hunters, collectors, criminals want guns.

No civilian needs such weaponry. Latest shooter
had numerous guns at several locations. Laws
are inadequate. How did he get them in the hotel?

Mental illness, extreme ideologies, various forms
of violence destabilize societies. Peaceful folks
are weary of protesting, shouting, seeing innocents die.

In Just October

My shoes nuzzle into the wet grass.
Pillow softens my chi chair.
It's chilly and sunny. Shadows stretch.

Two butterflies fly by and head
to the front yard where orange holly
berries ripen toward red.

A curled, crispy filbert leaf floats down
right before me. Five red windfall apples
form a Big Dipper on the lawn.

No birds on this watch. A wind gust
scatters more leaves, but three low limb
apples cling like a defiant fist.

The nation recovers from hurricanes
and a mass shooting. Tom Petty died.
Lots of dying and disaster to start this month.

Nobel Prize astronomers finding ripples
in the universe is back page section A.
news. They spotted gravitational waves!

This is an advanced theory achieved with
ingenious equipment. A new way to observe
the cosmos and the front page news is grim.

They claim these gravitational waves will be
powerful ways for humanity to explore
the universe. But attention is focused earthbound.

These waves go through everything, even us. They
carry information on them astronomers could not
get otherwise–hope to learn how universe came to be.

Einstein theorized gravitational waves, but did not
think technology could detect tiny wobbles,
smaller than a piece of an atom.

"The waves are like a storm in the fabric
of space-time that is produced when two
black holes collide," said Kip Thorne.

The first detection came from a crash 1.3
billion light-years away and a light year
is about 5.88 trillion miles. Mind-boggling.

The waves are detected with a laser device
called an interferometer. It cost $1.1 billion.
First observation: two devices 1,900 miles apart,

located at Hanford, Washington (just a state
away) and Livingston, Louisiana. They came
about 7 millisecond apart- the speed of light.

The Nobel winners were in their 70s and 80s-
Rainer Weiss, Barry Barish and Kip Thorne.
They pushed for years to start the LIGO project.

The Laser Interferometer Gravitational-wave Observatory
found a new way to probe the hidden recesses
of space, time and the universe.

The Nobel committee called it "a discovery that
shook the world." This wrinkle in fabric of space-time
released more energy than all stars in the universe!

Sure it was tinier than an atomic nucleus by the time
it reached us, but the detectors caught the feeble quiver.
They are revolutionizing astrophysics!

It took 1.3 billion years to reach Earth.
All this stellar achievement gets back page
after upheavals and deranged not genius minds.

It took two decades until the detector
was precise enough to succeed. A team
of 1000 astronomers observed waves in 2015.

Do people have enough time to get it right?
Can we be responsible or sustainable enough to survive
or will we return our real estate to the cosmos?

The Nobel Prize was announced just days after
traumatic earthly events. I look up at the wondrous
hidden universe, obscured by Gaia's clouds and sigh.

Land of the Elderberries

Once the Missoula Flood covered the Willamette Valley,
displacing people here for possibly 15,000-18,000 years.
This spot is the Land of the Elderberries. Lots of camas too.

Chepenefu Kalapuya people inhabited The Marys River
Valley now Corvallis, Philomath and Wren, part of 27 tribes
in the restored Confederated Tribes of the Grand Ronde.

Right here where I sit in my backyard chair, Kalapuya
roamed for thousands of years until disease, broken
treaties and termination of tribal status decimated them.

Our family was here when their tribal rights to their land
was restored. Tribes are reviving languages, native foods,
gathering diverse traditions to rebuild their culture.

An addition to a cultural museum will open in the spring.
Spirit Mountain casino and Marys Peak, a Spirit Mountain
nourish the lives of the Confederate tribes.

We were here when the land returned to them and the tribes
worked cooperatively and harmoniously to preserve
their culture. After so much trauma, they deserve more peace.

They controlled fires to create abundant crops like tarweed.
Elk and salmon, sustained them. They were part of trade
down to San Francisco. They know how to care for the land.

The Marys River and valley were named Chepenefu which refers
to the place where the elderberry are gathered. I do not think
I ever saw one. We raise raspberries, blueberries, strawberries.

I need to learn more of this locale, I have seen elk and salmon.
Probably saw camas, but never tasted it. Diverse flora and fauna
once flourished here. Perhaps we can learn how from the tribes.

Think how recently things changed. Imagine all the thousands
of years this spot endured flood, fire, many tribes.
In awe, I sip water in the nippy, harvest air.

Indigenous People Day

Today Columbus' reputation is under siege. But those seeking to delegitimize the Genoan explorer's legacy may actually have a larger target in mind. Statues to Columbus and tributes to his achievements are in many ways proxies for the Western tradition of freedom, liberty and the rule of law. Angela Rocco

As I sit and think to the tinkle of wind-chimes,
I wear a Southwest indigenously designed tee-shirt
under a blue hoodie with a tree of souls on the back.

I never thought Columbus deserved such acclaim.
Vikings came before him, if you only count Europeans.
I honor the native people here for thousand of years.

Columbus was on a voyage of exploitation to finance
the liberation of the Holy Land from Muslim domination,
spread the word of God and find a sea route to Asian trade.

He never stepped foot in North America, but the Caribbean.
He did not achieve his hoped for destination.
He introduced diseases which decimated the locals.

Columbus started the onslaught of Europeans, began
colonization, infections, slaughter, broken treaties for stolen
land, reservations, cultural appropriation and domination.

Just because Europeans could not travel to Asia because
of Muslim control of trade route, they sent explorers to find
a sea route, a new land was a bonus for burgeoning populations.

Just because only oldest son could inherit, they had a population
boom, because more mothers survived in childbirth and children survived,
population pressures sent Europeans emigrating-- natives sacrificed.

Europeans then moved on to exploit slaves and Asians.
Women were property-- so founders–white males–were
winners and perpetrators of racism, sexism and xenophobia.

We are still dealing with Columbus's legacy today despite
some improvements in women's and civil rights. We exploit
minorities in our wars for oil and greed, destroy land, air and sea.

With billions of people we have to make some adjustments.
We can't live the indigenous lifestyle with so many people.
We endure wealth inequities, crowding, pollution, violence.

Columbus was just one of the cruel Europeans to claim
other people's land as theirs. US history is a tale of blood
in the pursuit of gold, treasure by basically greedy white guys.

Whites said "Go West Young Man" (of course not women).
"American Destiny". Just wipe out anyone in your way
and steal their lands. Take the best land and leave them dregs.

We still have the KKK and White Fascists carrying crosses
and torches, wearing white hoods and white gowns or blatantly
unmasked and garbed more modernly, but thrusting tiki torches.

We have a lunatic leader (who is not my president)
and a NRA and lobby-bought Congress proposing walls,
bans, ending DACA, ways to keep diversity out.

America is not great yet. It will not be great until
freedom, liberty and rule of law applies to all
not just to wealthy, mostly white male privilege.

Arrivederci, Christopher Columbus-- time to heal,
repent as a nation all the horrendous acts you
are credited of unleashing. You just jump-started it.

Now some cities are renaming the federal holiday
Indigenous People Day. People put red paint
on the hands of your statue. "Hate will not be tolerated."

Perhaps someday marches will not be needed,
athletes will not have to kneel to protest injustice to blacks,
Italians will feel American without Columbus hype.

It is diversity that makes Americans so innovative,
so culturally rich. Perhaps someday we will achieve
the highest ideals supposedly founding our country.

The best in us comes by cooperating in disasters.
What about connecting in peace and harmony?
Climate change is coming with more immigrations globally.

Our constitution needs updates in electoral college,
gun control, gender equality, the list goes on and on.
Columbus could join the discredited Confederates.

The victims of European domination need to recognize
perspectives change over time, empires rise and fall.
USA is more likely to survive on strength of diversity.

For me, I recognize the first people to settle here.
The indigenous tribes whose wisdom and revival
is so needed, especially in this misguided time.

Full Moon in Aries

Apparently yesterday was not just a bad day,
but a full moon in Aries was on display
impacting us all forcefully, astrologists say.

Apparently the moon was most intense of this year,
causing fatigue, diminishing cheer.
Things felt worse than they appear.

Apparently I was not alone
to wake up and to grunt and groan.
I ached deep in muscle and bone.

Apparently if I knew I might take less seriously
the morning Trump news I treat derisively.
Meditate to calm me from one who acts imperiously?

Apparently when I went to exercise class,
any downer chatter would annoy me, alas
I could only hope my gloom would pass.

Apparently not right time for acupuncture,
wound up tight, stress not released from punctures.
Needle in head spouted blood, but needed no suture.

Apparently the moon followed me where I went,
I decided no more acupuncture event.
I received the omen the cosmos sent.

Apparently from this draining mishap,
I tiredly needed a restorative nap.
Mid-afternoon changed with a snap.

Then cooperative Scrabble players arrived.
With our word-play and laughter I revived
and with a blue lapis lazuli angel gift I received.

Then welcomed house guests and we went to dinner.
Hubby and I treated - good but I'm not thinner.
The day was turning from loser to winner.

Then when the moon glowed in the dark,
a bookstore poetry reading ignited a spark.
The evening ends on a high mark.

Then my purse left in a car required a switch.
But considering today, but a minor glitch.
The moon was shadowed by a witch?

Then when all but me went to bed.
I went and wrote a poem instead,
until pillow received a heavy head.

Apparently through day moon lost its grip.
Some incidents I'll just let slip,
but I'm ready for some Serendip.

Today with massage I feel lighter.
My chakras, attitude and mood--much brighter.
I'll prepare for the next full moon-blighter.

A Clean Slate

After recent-hour-shower I risk
going into the backyard for chi-time.
Shadows waver in and out.

I carry a blue pillow to place on the wet
metal chair, sit stiffly to avoid my arms
touching the rain-speckled chair arms.

I wear my hoodie over my head
under a quilted jacket. It is damp.
It is cold. Intermittent sun is not warming.

Raindrops glisten and drip from leaves.
Grass wiggles, soggy leaves twitch
from wind-wavelets down to my feet.

Each day fewer fruit-falls. Today
the count is three windfall apples
and one golden, grounded pear.

Each day smaller and less birds.
Haven't seen a butterfly in about a week.
Hoses removed and coiled.

Still the reddish-pink of the neighbor's
tall tree pokes through-- a splotchy backdrop
to our balding Macintosh.

Wimpy wind can't provoke wind-chimes.
How much longer will I chi-slurp outside,
shivering, yearning for flashes of color?

Time for a clean slate? Go inside
our enclosed outdoor moon room?
Meditate touching green slate floor?

I could bring a space heater.
I could leave a fold-able, comfortable dry chair.
I could be protected from the weather.

I carry the pillow inside. The dampened bottom
has the web pattern of the chair seat, even
though I had swiped the seat with my hand.

Will this be my last 2017 backyard
chi-gathering session? Will I begin
a clean slate on green slate?

I need to remain grounded, nourish
my root chakra, loop my chi, meditate
and stir my muse in my backyard.

It has been four and one-half months
of changing scenarios and intentions.
This October I'm supposed to look inward.

I can look inward anywhere. Slate
sticks to ground. I can move to higher
ground when I sit inside my living room.

Can I thrust my thoughts and chi
through enough layers above
and below me to connect the loop?

I have made these changes before.
The renewal of my chi grounding
practice this summer was very rewarding.

I will miss my rusty angel, Airlika. She will
hang further away. Bottom, the dirt-encrusted angel
lolls on my blue table beside me outdoors.

I look forward to spring when I can
green with the backyard, hopefully
bloom in fertile soil, touch angels.

Deep Breathing

Fall chill prods me to leave eave-shade,
carry a chair to center of backyard
under the rusty angel hanging on a hazelnut branch.

My back is to the sun. Chi warms,
as I absorb it through my feet and head.
I begin deep breathing practice.

Inhale–hold–exhale–hold
repeat until the gaps supposedly
fill with meditation, tranquilize me.

I can breathe as deeply as I can
for as long as I want, but I focus
outward, not inward, get distracted.

With no filberts left, the birds
peck bark for bugs and borers
on other trees while I am present.

One dandelion in full yellow glow,
another gray whiskers ready to blow,
punctuate the grass along with windfall apples.

Macintosh apples still abundant, ripen
with remnant pears. Soon our bountiful
harvest will be gone. Leaf-fall shrivels.

My deep breathing turns thoughts inward,
to chilling news of wildfires, hurricane recovery,
questioned credibility, stolen credit information.

Millions in peril from many causes.
I huff and puff in smokeless blue sky,
clutch mobile phone; only wind chimes ring.

With a sigh, I watch wind-wiggling shadows,
haul the light chair to darkened space,
heave my heavy hulk inside for lunch.

Shadowing

When I sit under the hazelnut tree
with my back to the sun, gathering chi,
I hope the sun warms my sore neck.

I manage to face the trunk
with its mossy, lumpy bark,
so the front of me is in shade.

My shadow interlaces with the tree's
canopy shade. Mine stationary.
The hazelnut's shadow dances in breeze.

My featureless shadow is solid dark.
The hazelnut's splotchy with light spots.
I could be Buddha. But the tree—could be most any tree.

I wonder if I could make my shadow
look more skinny in another position
or another time of day?

The sleek, shadow-splattered, rusty angel
nearby flies west against little headwind
hangs beneath leaf-clouds.

The sun does not penetrate
my tee shirt or my bare neck—
at least enough for pain relief.

How long should I wait for autumn's arrival
where things get chilly and moisten?
This might be my last chance to sun-heal for awhile.

I sun-soak with hope, then head inside
for the heating pad. My shadow follows
as long as it can, wobbling like wind-shade.

Seeing Red

For months I've stared at a red stain
on the center of three thick branches
under the leafy layers of main apple trunk.

This red swathe could not be rust,
though similar in shade to rusty angel
swaying under a hazelnut limb nearby.

It is not blood even though birds peck
all over the branches and not smooth
flowing or shiny like sap.

The branches on both side favor
a variegated green, hue–scraggly textured,
moss or fungi– no reddish strands.

Since my distant vision is not acute,
I walked over to the middle section
and discovered a soft, cushiony growth.

Clustered, bubblets–more subdued bloom
to the gangly green gangs surrounding it.
But why just that one splotch on one tree?

This section has two tumor-like protrusions.
The other two branches–have scar-like holes
like puckered lips. Maybe portals?

Perhaps–three branches symbolize
the three siblings in my family tree?
I am the sister between two brothers.

Maybe my three children or grandchildren?
Both sets have one girl and two boys.
Triplet family sets. Tri-fork. My tree trident.

Whatever, it is bark textured in red and green
overlooking windfall apples on grass--
calming not angry red in a green view.

Rooted in the earth, this festive display
illustrates connectedness, if nothing else,
and somehow warms hope.

Backyard in Autumn

raindrops glisten on leaves
drip on crispy fallen leaves
autumnal tears

clouds shroud shadows
drain rain on cracked earth, green brown spots
puff and flatten

Behind
stripping apple
limbs, neighbor's reddish-pink
leaves flesh out backstage like blushing
fig leaves.

Good-bye
dandelions–
you're not a weed to me–
sunspots in scraggly lawn before
butch-cut.

One plum,
and few peaches,
some pears and more apples,
raspberries, blue and strawberries
soon gone.

apples' spindly stems
cling to encrusted branch
defy blustery wind

raccoons
crunch our apples,
avoid our windfall pears,
gnaw big bite, leave un-bitten skin
witchly.

Orange harvest sun
Halloween masks, tinges the yard
spreads sunsets

Preparing for Rain

My husband interrupts his reel mowing
to shout inside to me if I wanted to gather chi
I'd better come out before it rains.

He has picked up windfall apples, four pears,
installed cinder block steps, pulled some weeds
before attacking the brown, meager grass.

The grass did not need mowing. Fissures
crack ground from lack of rain. But he wants
to get the mower repaired before greening rain.

The westerly wind brings a chill as the sun
hides behind clouds and removes shadows.
Rain is on its way. Last night's smoke fled.

He covered my black metal chair with a shower
curtain- colorful fish swim on clear vinyl,
held in place by two bricks and large clips,

an encouragement to sit between storms
and not get wet. He suggested maybe a cushion.
My chair-tent could lengthen my time with chi.

He sits across from me on the cinder block step
and seat proclaiming he also found strawberries
and raspberries to snack on. No birds in sight.

We look over the yard to see what we might
have missed and not prepared for when rain
arrives and hopefully helps firefighters.

This is the lull before the storm, wind-whisks
sweep away lingering smoke. It feels like fall.
I shiver in my nightgown and stocking feet.

Time's up for soaking in chi. Brief shadows sprawl
across the tightly cropped lawn. I re-cover the chair.
On the table a small, dirty concrete angel faces a bath.

My husband pushes the mower to the garage
after picking up his tools. The hanging, rusty angel,
is exposed to further crustiness, when the rain arrives.

Autumnal Appraisal

After a week of spurning chi chair sessions
I return to the backyard on a sunny, warmish
day at near-noon. I'm a fair-weather outdoor fan.

I remove the chair covering, plunk a pillow.
My red cape over my hoodie flows
over my limbs like leaves on a branch.

I assess what has changed since last look.
Three low apples still cling. One un-munched windfall.
Red-pink tree behind lacy apple tree creates mosaic.

No other fruit or berries remain.
Leaves flurry to ground with every breeze
to wind-chime accompaniment.

Near the grave of the cherry tree are clusters
of white mushrooms with a patina, peppered
like with dirt or brown sprinkles on a cupcake.

Eight mushrooms line up together
with a smaller one below like a period
at the bottom of an exclamation point.

Two rub sides. Two others remain single.
Not sure if they are poisonous or not.
No creature seems to bite them.

I do not like mushrooms, so they're safe with me.
I'll let them be- spots of color like dandelions
in the still- green lawn littered with leaves.

No birds, bugs, butterflies,
squirrels, cats, deer, raccoons
pecking and chomping tidbits.

I dyed hair blue/purple/pink.
Tomorrow is supposed to rain.
Dye might dribble down my face.

My dye job is temporary and will fade in a few weeks.
My almost-white locks should return--omen of snow
or blue sky clouds? Will I wait inside and see?

Conjuring Witches

Life is valuable–when completed by the imagination and then only.
William Carlos Williams

A week before Halloween my backyard is spooky.
Two spectral dandelion puffs are ready to poof. One red leaf
shines among grounded, browned hazelnut and apple leaves.

No windfall apples and less than a dozen
left on their limbs. Crusty bark, shadowed
with sun-splotches, blisters gnarly.

The witches' ring of mushrooms are clustered
ghosts, gray with a charcoal rim. Limp and lifeless.
Dewdrops twinkle in the sunlight–wand-sparks.

Two tan new mushrooms stretch under
the hazelnut tree, blend with slippery moist leaves.
Magical mushroom tops appear cinnamon-sprinkled.

I am the most colorful object in the yard with my
blue/purple/pink Halloweeny hair. The remaining
red/purple apples are too dark and dull for a witchy trick.

But Airlika, my rusty hanging angel, might be lonely
and tooting her horn to invite witches to visit from another
dimension on drones or old-fashioned broomsticks.

Unseen, the garden devas relax, the fairies
stash umbrella leaves, dance to wind-chimes
flutes and fiddlesticks. Maybe music apps?

The colors are fading, fruit harvested, yet
underground worms tunnel, slimey slugs slink.
What temperature is my chi brew? From a witch's stew?

Memories haunt, imagination conjures seasonal
myths and magic. I can update witches' garb–
to jumpsuits, switch a black cat for a handsome hologram.

As I sit in my chi chair juicing up my energy,
I wander off in wonder to dream places, become
a good witch, using my wand to transform Gaia.

Halloween Haunts

I tell you it has taken me all my life to arrive at the vision of gas lamps as angels,
to soften the blur and finally banish the edges you regret I don't see.
Lisel Mueller "Monet Refuses the Operation."

Yesterday's fog cleared and today
all the stealthy specters and gauzy ghosts
will have clear haunting.

I sit in my chilly chi chair appreciating
the sun and shadows foreshadowing
expected bleary rain tomorrow.

When my husband mowed the lawn,
he dug up any magical mushrooms, curdled
leaves replace those he raked.

Only three apples for witches to use.
No other fruits to poison. Do creatures
lurk in the yard this spooktacular day?

My glasses need cleaning. My vision
blurs like late Monet. My cataracts not ripe
enough for surgery, unlike his.

I wonder what Monet's blurry ponds
would look with my deteriorating sight--
add fingerprints or smears on glasses.

I mix up my glasses- long distance
when reading, vice-versa. My confused eyes
wonder what edges and boundaries disappeared.

I can visualize imaginary sights, blended dimensions,
lines for counties, states, nations often unseen,
in this fuzzy world blurring differences.

When the veil is thin, supernatural beings
transform density, transparency vacillates,
mystical realms seem possible.

All these essences exist in possibility.
Which bridges can we cross? Which
consciousness' can connect, meld?

Exiting October

As we exit October, colors mute, branches bare.
In the distance a tall tree with red leaves
flames over the top of our back fence.

A neighbor's red tree- a backdrop to our apple
has mellowed yellow-orange from red-pink,
while apple limbs brown and strip.

The few apples I can spot are purple, cling
don't drop. The two new mushrooms'
umbrellas deflate and develop an edge ring.

The cluster of decaying, gray mushrooms look
like donkey ears. Beige leaves need raking.
Birds are in the front yard, not here.

Our organic harvests are meager in the back,
but red-ripe holly berries await out front.
Untainted by chemicals, are they safe to eat?

Chemicals cause contaminated air and pollute
water globally at an alarming rate. Nations
dispute climate change and regulations.

Millions of people die, become unproductive,
less reproductive, contract diverse diseases.
We genetically damage our children.

Unless we care for the planet, we cannot
care for ourselves. The news is dire.
We lack effective leadership for change.

As we see people abdicate personal
responsibility, integrity and community duty,
the chaos leads us to ponder our viability.

All the bad news overwhelms the efforts
of kind, generous, creative people to serve.
Arts and sciences struggle to bring light.

It is afternoon as I sit and slurp in chi.
Is energy for our life force compromised also?
How can our consciousness rise to the challenges?

Mutually Blue

A chilly day after Halloween the skies are blue,
with scowling gray skies to the west as predicted.
I'm disappointed we had only four trick or treaters.

I did not expect to be able to sit on my blue pillow
in my chi chair perusing the backyard. I expected
dampened spirits after a clear haunting eve.

Crunchy leaves cover the lawn like apple crisp.
A lower limb apple turns dark purple as if bruised.
Wind-chimes knell in vigorous wind.

My thoughts drift to an upbeat, blue moment.
Blue evokes contemplation, an invitation
to create, explore the great blue yonder.

On the way to lunch with Maureen, we saw
a blue heron blocked by the roadside fence.
We gaped in awe and admiration.

Both of us are temporarily tinted with blue hair.
Did the heron notice our blue locks?
Did he turn his head as we drove by?

A touch of blue in heavy times is a hint
of hope and joy. We broadcast bright blue vibes.
We three are blue birds of a feather.

Uplifted in spirit, we drove to our lunch
to celebrate her birthday, finishing *Mirabilia*
and beginning *Spiral Hands* collaboration.

Seeing surprising omens connects us
to wider horizons, reminds us we are part of All,
especially when we see blue with wings.

Full Moon in Taurus

It's full moon in Taurus a very auspicious day
according to my masseuse. I sit in the backyard
gathering chi amid a raindrop sprinkled lawn.

The underside of the spiraled green hose glistens
with raindrops, like lights on a Christmas tree.
The chair tarp pimpled with rain drops, clears.

Grounded leaves cuddle closer. The maple
red backdrop for the apple tree is gone.
A blue jay pecks filbert tree bark, barren of nuts.

This is supposed to be a very good day–
especially by tonight about ten–maybe
even a clear view. Rain tomorrow?

Yesterday I had a nap-mare, a scary
post Halloween screamer when I could
not yell my fear of the coming onslaught.

I remember a tall metal wall–30-50 feet.
Some knobs like the flat front of a machine,
powering toward me, without sound.

I was on the ground–horizontal to it,
trying to roll out of the way and be heard
so it would stop. Real heebie-jeebies.

I woke up before crunched in its maw.
Not sure the symbolism. Trump's wall?
Some approaching alien invasion?

Scraping off Earth's surface to rebuild?
Who would be the builders?
Symbolic of some obstacle I'm facing?

Whatever, my masseuse said no clouds
over my head and my chakras are cleansed
and balanced. Should be safe to nap this fine day.

The rain spits at me to retreat inside.
I cover the chi chair tarp and carefully, I
optimistically head to the couch to nap.

Downcast

On an overcast late morning I sit in the backyard
on my chilly, chi- gathering, metal chair.
I forgot to bring my warm, soft, blue pillow.

Small dark birds nip bark in apple and filbert
canopies. Only two apples cling to their limb.
The leaf crowd nestles closer, splotch the lawn.

Ten clusters of white mushrooms–in groups
of three-to-ten arc the damp grass. One quartet
huddles near the wall. Lovely sheen contrast.

The large mushrooms are like planets with smaller
ones orbiting moons. The large tops--sprinkled
with cinnamon pocks. Very irregular patterns.

Ten larger mushrooms smoosh together
with tiny satellites. White dots splatter
in the leaf-covered lawn, expand territory.

My mind drifts to the shooting in a Texas church
by an assault-rifle-carrying, young white man.
He did not have a gun license even.

Just the latest mass shooter with a war weapon.
White men are getting some bad press exposure:
White Supremacists, sexual harassment, violence...

A depressed student at M.I.T. committed suicide.
The parents sue the school. Who's responsible
for the student's mental health? Fatal frat hazings?

Collusion with Russia implied to Trump,
his millionaire and billionaire cabinet
and cronies. More white men behaving badly.

Government not in best interests of even
the majority. Benefits, DACA, taxes in disarray.
Their approval polls very low. Serving only rich.

Climate change, stealing National Park land,
destroying protections under incompetent departments
heads... Every day a blow to democracy and integrity.

No, I can't control events, but power-grubbers
reduce the quality of life for humanity,
destroy and diminish our planet for greed:

mass migrations, immigrant bans, extreme
poverty, mining, disease. People trapped in places
of contaminated water, polluted air–dying.

Land, sea and air struggle to sustain us.
We can be in the wrong place
at the wrong time–at events out of our control.

Some gurus say we should go with the cosmic
flow, pray for interventions, surrender
to God's will. Change what we can.

It is easy to be overwhelmed by the challenges,
hard to bear the losses, injustices, inequalities.
Dreams become nightmares even when awake.

Today the newscasters try to answer why
another deranged man slaughters 26 with a gun.
Recently, a terrorist in NYC killed 8 with a truck.

Will the disenfranchised of the world rise
to demand equity, sustainability and justice for all?
If they do in my lifetime, I stand with them.

As I cover the chair from the rain, I turn
for one more glance of the shadow-less yard.
Mushrooms beam like beacons of light.

Considering Change

Seasonal change is gradual and relentless,
moves sluggishly like Congress. I watch
as the backyard thrusts onward into winter.

I put up my hoodie, l carry my pillow
to warm the chilly, chi chair seat.
Hands in pockets, as I survey the yard.

Last night it was 32 degrees with frost.
Grocery store parking lot had de-icing--
white, sparkly bits on asphalt.

Daily the leaves reveal interlaced limb patterns,
gray-brown bark encrusted with lichen and moss.
Moss inches over the patio stones.

The white mushrooms appear stagnant.
I have no idea what type they are or care
as I do not like eating them. Live and let live.

We have had house guests with changes
in schedules and meals. It was not a difficult
adjustment. Change sometimes shakes things up.

As the four of us adapt to aging, priorities
change, more wisdom to our choices?
I do not want to become crusty like bark.

Our gray hair (except my hair is blue/purple/pink
at the moment) mirrors the grayness of sky,
rock wall, stone, and tree trunks and limbs.

We face change with some resilience.
We need to be courageous amid gray times.
Perhaps my dyed hair brightens prospects?

As I clutch the pillow and head indoors, I look
forward to rotating the heating pad on sore spots:
shoulders, knees, back, liver as I type away my pain.

Fairy Rings

Fairy rings also known as a fairy circle, elf circle, elf ring or pixie ring is a
naturally occurring ring or arc of mushrooms. The rings can grow to over ten
meters or 33 feet in diameter and they become stable over time as the fungus
grows to seek food underground. They are found mainly in forest areas, but also
appear in grasslands or rangelands. Wikipedia

Our fairy ring arcs near the mound
of the chopped down cherry tree. Maybe
the mushrooms feed on decaying roots?

The first few were dug up, but more arrived,
more abundantly. Now up to 15 clusters
from one - ten in a bulging semi-circle.

I always thought fairy circles were dance
rings- spritely folks dancing to fiddles or harps
to melodious strokes, leapt one to another.

But I read fairy rings can be hazardous,
places where you can be lured inside
their midst, deluded, crumbled to dust.

But the fairy circles can be places
of abundance, good fortune, music–
guess it depends on good or evil fairies?

In France they are called Sorcerer's Rings,
in German-- Witches Rings where they dance
on Walpurgis Night. The French rings are guarded

by a giant bug-eyed toad who curses miss-steppers.
Dutch rings are where the devil puts down a milk churn.
In the Tyrol the rings are fiery tails of flying dragons.

Scandinavian elfdans' dancing elves put intruders into
a thrall of illusions, but some folks claim to dance with them.
Fairies have long dance and music traditions.

Fairy villages spring underground the ring,
use mushrooms for parasols and umbrellas.
They like rings around hawthorn trees.

Don't dig them up for it is fruit less and bad luck.
Step in and you die young. A "galley-trap" hangs
thief or murderer. Could dance to exhaustion.

Fairies get befuddled by marjoram or thyme,
dislike iron, rowan sticks. Someone must
pull you out of a ring from the mortal world.

You may have no memory of your time there.
Time works slower in the outside world.
Maybe you married a fairy?

If you go widdershins trying to escape, fairies
can put runner under their enchantment. Also
don't circle ring ten times, could be ensnared.

If you wear your hat backwards, fairies
get confused. It could prevent you
from being pulled into their ring.

Some rings are places of fertility, fortune,
abundance. Some fairies dance around
a glow worm. People have reported dancing with them.

Fairy ring lore in literature and art is global.
The two Williams- Shakespeare and Blake,
fairy books by Brian Froud– I treasure.

I collect fairy art, fairy stories, miniature elves
and fairies. Fairy rings might just be showing
appreciation for my support of winged beings.

My fairies have a North American ring in a
suburban backyard in lush Northwest. They
are welcome as long as they want to enchant me.

Some day from the corner of my eye, I might spy
them dance and fly with garden devas clapping,
flowers and leaves swaying to the beat.

Plucking the Fairy's Eyebrow

Tightly crunched leaves almost hide
the mushroom fairy arc. My husband
dug the ends like a plucked fairy eyebrow.

Few have seen beyond the veil
the world of faerie. Hopefully if they
inhabit here, they are snug underground.

I am underdressed as I sit on a chilly chair
trying to loop chi from cosmos and ground.
When did chi, life force arrive in cosmic plan?

On Star Talk Neal deGrasse Tyson discussed
the origin of the universe and the more we know
the more the boundary of unknowing expands.

What was before the Big Bang? What about
the space the supposedly singularity sparked
into? What ignited the current unfolding? Others?

How did particles know to be energy, matter,
light? Dark energy and dark matter? Did
the Omnisparkler have a committee? Debate laws?

Math is part of cosmic language as is sound.
The immensity requires division of creative
ideation and many blueprints? Multiverse?

Time and space, space/time, sentience,
containers for consciousness and free range
souls without bodies–all on some unknown mission?

Which beings and creators do we hold responsible?
How accessible are higher beings in many realms?
The Earth Experiment is not passing the test.

Who will intervene or will we become extinct? Would
Gaia and our galaxy be better off without us, so they
can start again with starseeds filled with lighter starstuff?

What is our part in the cosmic scheme of things?
What are the roles of light-bringers, gods, scientists,
artists, creators of all sorts from food to computers?

I am cosmically curious. I am curious about
worlds I can imagine but not witness: angels,
fairies, lives beyond the veil, departed ones' fates.

In my dream (another source of fascination)
I was in a high school science class. The teacher
divided us into groups of five. My group had five girls.

Our topic was "How did the universe begin?"
Three girls said the Bible told us how it began.
Another girl was silent. I said no. We don't know.

I was afraid the report would be very lopsided.
The silent one said she would dump all ideas together.
I asked what sources was she considering?

Then it was the Bible-Thumpers and the Internet
cruncher against me who had no definitive answer.
I was on the scientific side of probing the origin question.

Spirituality and science both probe the unknown,
trying to transcend our human limitations and find
information how we can live our lives better.

Infinite complexity is part of All there is from the strand
in a fairy's eyebrow, sparticles, strange particles, sparkles
from stars, moons and planets, black holes, gravitational waves...

I do not expect to know in this lifetime how
this universe began, its intention and how it works.
But I am watching and wondering about All.

Noticing

Outside the front window the wind is briskly
flailing limbs wildly, camellia petals flutter
to join the tan leaves on the still green lawn.

Moss munches the sidewalk-chunked wall.
Beside the fire hydrant, the mail box waits to open
its maw. Our driveway littered with natural needles.

Red holly berries ready for the pecking.
The welcome to all sign bows in stiff breeze
and struggles to stay upright.

The metal and stone yard art figures
must be cold to the touch, glistening
in the afternoon sun watching passers-by.

Inside I see much of the outside world
through glass and on screens,
but still no smart or cell phone.

I contemplate going into the backyard
to stir up some chi, sitting on my chilling
chair, but I'd have to bundle up.

So the front yard view will have to do
today, feet on hard wood floors,
glassy-eyed, fewer layers for warmth.

In my hustle-bustle, distracted
younger days, I did not have or take
the time to notice my surroundings.

We took our children and grandchildren
on trips to museums and national parks,
played ball games and golf in the backyard.

But often I was watching them
and the background blurred in a flurry
of motion and sound.

Today I will notice the front yard
and inside the thousands of angels,
and seasonal decorations I whisk by.

Between Storms

Between rain and sun, drench and dry.
Between exercise class and massage
I risk sitting outside sipping chi.

The backyard is wet, dripping drops.
Muted or no shadows on lawn.
Blue skies cloud in a blink.

The fairy ring mushrooms shrivel,
ruffled edges brown like dirt.
Some crack. All lost their luster.

The breaking news is sexual harassment
by politicians, priests, pastors, predators
in business, entertainment–everywhere.

They prey on vulnerable teens,
aspiring applicants, children.
Men can't keep hands off, penis in pants.

Now that attacks against men as well
as women are revealed, maybe
we will get more attention to the issue.

Men in power take advantage,
disenfranchise, dis-empower others.
feel it is their male privilege.

Beliefs and cultural mores excuse
and forgive this travesty forgetting
the victims. Sorry, payoffs not enough.

We need a moral shift, mutual respect,
reduction of violence or we will continue
to live between storms, downpours of injustice.

What a Wimpy Rain!

Such a miserable dribble.
We have been waiting for days
for the advent of fall rains—
for this?

Not enough rain to speckle a skylight.
Not enough to sprinkle on wildfires.
Not enough to wet my socks through.
Not this.

The ground cracks did not moisten.
The grass no more inkling of green.
The sidewalks look pretty pristine.
For this?

Not enough for coastal winds to bother.
Not enough for metal to rust.
Not enough to tamp the smoke.
Not this.

The sky is gray, smudged with smoke.
The air does not feel fresh or rain-heavy.
The yard has an orange tinge before sunset.
For this?

I wanted a skylight splasher with rain pings.
I wanted soggy ground, perky dandelions.
I wanted slippery sidewalks, shiny streets.
Not this.

The World Did Not End

Well, we managed to avoid another apocalypse.
Today is a sunny Sunday with a slight chill.
The predictors can go to their church in gratitude.

The holly berries are an autumnal orange.
Leaves reddening, tanning, dropping.
A raccoon crunched two windfall apples.

A stellar jay shakes the rhododendron.
On the sidewalk chunk wall, a small brown
LBJ about half jay-size snoops around.

Grass is filling in the brown spots.
Wind-chimes barely clink
in the chilly, wimpy wind.

Solid roof shadows sprawl.
Tree tracery flows on lawn.
Muted colors and sounds.

The yard is more like a still life.
I miss the bird chatter, snacking and flights.
I miss chime clangs and apple plops.

I miss the butterfly solos,
dandelions of any hue.
I even miss the lollygagging cat.

If I am to gather daily chi in these conditions,
my focus will be diverted inward.
Will my root chakra get nourished enough?

Will I end up a fair-weather witness?
Peer at the world through windows
and screens, not grounding?

I must maintain a balance
of inner and outer stimulus.
I'll start by wearing my red cape outside.

Bluetiful

I stand at the window where
the world ends, barely breathing
reciting a poem to myself
I believe in this ordinary day.
A day I can still make it outdoors alive.   Ann Emerson

I contemplate long-sleeves to slurp up chi.
As I open the door to the backyard,
fast food lunch in hand, I think of Cassini
diving into Saturn in a spectacular splash,
and other dramatic/traumatic headlines of the day.

But...a new brilliant blue hue from OSU
was named a new crayon color by Crayola.
Scientists at Oregon State University
accidentally discovered it while experimenting
with materials to use in electronics.

Bluetiful won over 90,000 submissions.
Dreams Come Blue, Blue Moon Bliss,
Reach for the Stars and Star Spangled Blue
were other top five contenders.
Bluetiful will replace retiring Dandelion.

Bluetiful's pigment does not fade. Crayola
has a promotional page just for Bluetiful.
It includes the crayon's hobbies (coding apps)
and pet causes (STEM education). Lead researcher
Max Subramanian picked his favorite name on Twitter.

On newsprint it is hard to tell its true hue.
My rainbow tee's blue or jeans' blue
do not match. The sky is too faded today.
Too milky with clouds. Too pastel.
My favorite color is blue no matter what shade.

In my yard there is still a dandelion basking
beneath the sun. Not a weed to me
but a drop of sunshine under an anemic blue sky.
We need more bluetiful in this muted world--
so everything is bluetiful in its own way.

44

Inner Peace

Yet inner peace by its definition isn't based on outer events. It's a way of looking at things, a way of perception. And most importantly: it is a way of understanding our true nature as infinite beings. Sara Wiseman

A brisk breeze dances shadows across the lawn.
One windfall apple looks shiny as if licked by a raccoon,
peed on by a cat or slobbered over by a dog.

I carry a mobile phone and pillow into the backyard
to receive an important call while seated comfortably.
I am anxious for the call. Some issues unsettled.

Leaves fall. Only a few apples grounded.
No squirrels or birds flitting about.
The agitation is all within me. Unblock flow chi.

Supposedly, we can begin to create inner peace
by connecting to the Universe more often.
Are there devices to connect? Who do you dial?

Supposedly, we can begin to create inner peace
by understanding we are all souls.
I understand this, but this is not very reassuring.

Supposedly we can begin to create inner peace
by meditation, prayer, stillness, nature.
I have tried all these techniques, but I am not tranquil.

Supposedly we can begin to create inner peace
if we connect to this beautiful frequency or vibration.
Apparently I am getting a busy signal?

The more attuned to this level of consciousness
or understanding, the more infused we are to this frequency,
the more we live there all the time. I'm on call waiting?

We experience peace so we see things more peacefully.
So we experience more peace. So far I am not in the loop.
Perhaps I am just experiencing technical difficulties?

Supposedly what we pay attention to expands.
This is true of spiritual practice. Snowball peace
so more peace enters your reality. No snow this season.

Meanwhile, I sit amid falling foliage. Silent phone
on small blue table beside me. A concrete angel
about phone-size soaks shade backside down.

I receive a request call for a ride to a poetry reading
tonight. Then the relieving call to meet this afternoon.
I am calmed down. More inner peace but...

there is so much tumult transpiring in the world.
My local anxiety was minimal. If I have a hard time
handling the small stuff...what chance have I with wider picture?

Under Turbulent Clouds

Under turbulent clouds I sit in the backyard
for my daily dose of chi, but after months of sun,
no shadows, no warmth–heavy air.

This weekend Portland was awash in pink
as people marched for a cancer cure.
Juggalos, pro and anti-Trump marchers in D.C.

Mall protesters marched against not guilty
verdict for a white cop accused of killing
a black man in St. Louis. Facebook fraud.

Ken Burn's documentary on Viet Nam began
with revelations of deceit on all sides.
At the Emmy's many wore blue ribbons for ACLU.

Turmoil in the sky and on land. Cassini's demise,
drones under scrutiny, air travel unpleasant,
hurricanes, wildfires, pollution ramping up.

Global unease with situations seeming out of control.
So much fear and frustration as autumn darkens.
I ponder the ominous outlook.

A blitz of sun casts momentary shadows.
A spit of rain hits my hand.
Leaves do not cradle raindrops...yet.

At my feet a light-green lacy lichen,
like a snowflake cuddles close
to a bruised red windfall apple--

a calming tableau as the winds gust.
I need to end this reverie and go inside
where I left my jacket–my protective warmth.

A Real Rain

Just before the fall equinox we get a real rain.
A gully washer in the gorge caused landslides,
first snow in the Cascades, flash floods, tornadoes.

In three days I went from short sleeves to long sleeves
to sweat shirt. Yesterday we had our welcome
thunderstorm, tamping wildfires, flushing smoke.

Slick sidewalks and streets, raindrops glisten
on leaves, slither down the shower curtain covering
my chi chair, rinse windfalls, plop on my head.

Intermittent shadows cross on the lawn
as sun peeks through scowly clouds,
heavy laden for later rainfall.

I go inside to get ready to go to lunch with friends
and ride a carousel. I will need a warm jacket.
Time to enjoy a respite before the next storm.

Nap-Zapper

For the third day, a noisome bombardier
dive-bombed both ears, encircled my head,
landed on my shoulder, cheek and hand.

The buzz and swatting, woke me up
from a well-deserved nap. My husband
has been chasing a fly harassing him also.

Groggily, I get up- with a husband hand-assist.
Stuff into a cumbersome coat, to energize
with some backyard chi–chilly chi.

I earned that nap. Last night I stayed up until
midnight enduring Vietnam documentary, enjoying
Colbert's monologue, correcting my book proof.

This morning I showered, went to exercise class,
bought groceries, finally got a haircut, ate
breakfast and lunch and read three newspapers.

Grumpily, I sat on the chair mumbling about
my interrupted nap to the blemished windfall apples,
when I spotted two apples had big bites.

I reported this find to my husband, who inspected
the two throw-aways, blaming raccoons, who
do not respect boundaries–like flies.

He picked up about a dozen more–sorting
Macintosh from Delicious in storage bins.
The Delicious last longer. A raindrop spits at me.

As I am about to go inside, sun shadow-splotches
the lawn. It was a brief, but hopeful omen maybe
my afternoon endeavors won't bomb.

The Angel Weathervane

On overcast, rainy Thanksgiving Day
between storms my husband installed
a gift angel weathervane in the backyard.

He rented a hand truck to move the hefty angel.
She sits on the eastern side of the sidewalk
chunked wall near spindly barren azaleas.

She appears to be tooting a horn as I gaze
at her through a window. She is a patina-ed
metal above a weathervane with NEWS on ends.

She is attached to a heavy concrete block
which slopes like a decapitated pyramid--
a humongous pimple on the chunky gray wall.

All blends gray today, perhaps in sun shining
or wind-whirling she will get our attention better.
I'll call her Tootsie. Hope she does blow a horn.

The same friend gave me Airlika, a rusty
angel hanging on hazelnut branch and Bottom,
a reclining cement angel on the outdoor table.

My friend was moving and knew I collect angels.
She also gave me a solar clear plastic angel for a window
which rotates colors in the dark. I call her Rainbow.

Inside and outside I am surrounded by over
3000 angels. I am grateful for the angels,
friends and family who help me gather them.

Tootsie Toots Her Horn

The day after Thanksgiving is sunny.
I decide to sit in the backyard to draw in chi.
My chi chair has a pile of leaves on the seat.

I walk across the lawn to see if my new angel
weathervane, I named Tootsie, does indeed
have a horn. She does and directions are on target.

Her gray metal does not shine. She's muted.
She blends with sturdy concrete base.
She'll withstand strong storms.

Toostie has a shadow stripe behind her head.
Puffy white clouds race above her as if chased
by thunderclouds. Tootsie toots northwest.

I notice the fairy ring is gone. The mushrooms
turned brown and died, buried in the compost pile.
The dead cherry tree mound sprouts green whiskers.

Leaves mat thick and wet on the ground.
Only one hazelnut tree still clutches tan leaves.
No apples clinging. No fruit anywhere.

Birds still flit about. Perhaps it is time now
to fill the bird feeder since all the crops
have been harvested.

Moss and lichen encrust the fruit trees.
Bundling up for the cold? No leaves to nurture.
Rusty angel Airlika has lost her cover.

Both angels toot westerly– silent sentinels
to protect the backyard inhabitants, signals
of connections with higher realms.

The Silence Breakers

As I sit inhaling chi on a chilly, sunny morning
the backyard is still littered with leaves
as we approach the festivals of light season.

An inversion layer creates an air hazard, oppresses
breath. A lone bird calls to no response.
Wind-chimes tickled, but wimpy wind will not move air.

The stagnant air makes me reflect on unrelenting pressures
upon women who deal with boundary-breakers globally–
men who do not respect or protect women's integrity.

Times' Person of the Year was The Silence Breakers,
women whose voices launched a movement to speak out
against sexual assault and harassment– bullying balls.

The Women's whisper network has endured a long time--
before my mother confided she was harassed
by the principal where she taught. She did not yield.

Before my aunt who was a talented opera singer,
fended off men who ended her opportunities to singers
less talented, but accepted going along to get along.

Before the Women's Rights movement. Before Betty Friedan.
Before the Women's March. Before recorded history,
males made power grabs at women's expense.

Women are gaining strength and refusing to play along.
Women are uniting like consciousness raising groups,
on-line with sites like #MeToo and off shoots.

Will millions become billions-- lift the veil of cultural
and religious restraints and gain political and workplace power
until all people are treated with respect, kindness, equally?

I protect my boundaries. When frat boys tried to spike my
diet drink-- they failed. I outran a man who chased me.
I confront offensive language and male lewd behavior.

I refuse to remain silent as others are hurt.
I will persist and resist male oppression with my Huddle.
How do these men face their partners, mothers and sisters?

Perhaps now that women are speaking up
and standing their ground, cultural change will come?
Remember the women who withheld sex for peace?

Women can empower–take their power back
for a new age of justice and equality. Without hope
human civilization will crumble, split apart.

I have always been resentful of male privilege,
their domination over women's lives, their crushing
of women's spirits and opportunities.

Earth has so many challenges, requiring cooperation
from everyone to survive. If we can't change, perhaps
we should not populate Gaia with a failed experiment?

As I sit absorbing shadowed light, my chi looping
through me cosmos to Gaia–I dream women will come out
of the shadows to shine brilliantly with everyone.

I Stand At the Window

A few days before Christmas
I stand at the window to look
at the wet, cold backyard.

The moldy trees look like Jack Frost
scratched the bark and left scars,
on gangly, barren encrusted limbs.

Near the spot of the former cherry tree
there is a natural ring– a leafhenge
memorial. Most leaves swept away.

The durable angels are soaked:
weathervane Tootsie, hanging, rusty,
Airlika and laid back on small table, Bottom.

I do not want to go into the backyard.
Squishy ground, chilled chair.
Windowpane dribbles rain.

Perhaps for months now I'll stand
at the window on slate floor. Chi
will have to work harder to reach me.

Through the front windows, holiday
light showers dance through to the ceiling--
red and green sparks--festive fireflies.

As long as I am window-watching I will
enjoy sitting watching light showers for as long
as I can-- until sun and warmth return outside.

Mining Creative Gaps

I am an open channel for creative ideas.

Louise Hay

Seasonal Characters

What do the mythical characters
in our holidays and celebrations do
on their off-season? These actors
relax, resume planning, create hullaballoo?
        Around the year they have roles to play.
        I wonder where they are this World Peace Day?

In our holidays and celebrations do
they consider upgrading their gear and mission?
Are they satisfying characters to you?
If they modernize, do they want permission?
        Some folks don't give up old ideas well.
        But then some might–who can tell?

On their off season, these actors
prepare for their spotlight season?
What is the mood of these enactors?
Do they need another reason
        to perform their customary tasks?
        Who goes to work and who basks?

Relax, resume planning, create hullaballoo?
Easter bunnies decorate eggs, procreate?
Santas head south to sunny Kallamazoo?
Thanksgiving creatures might try to re-negotiate.
        Witches' covens make cauldron brew?
        Maybe switch to stew, fondue or ragout?

Around the year they have roles to play.
Santas, witches, Pilgrims, try more flashy fashion?
Leprechauns add electronics in present day?
Bunnies, for environment, curb their passion?
        Rather than making humans happy, instead,
        they might make life sustainable for living, not dead.

I wonder where they are this World Peace Day?
Are they amping up harmonic ways or global turmoil?
Their messages and methods in disarray?
Universal appeal? More calm, less roil?
        Where are new role models for this turbulent year
        to make our disillusions disappear?

The Witch Bitches About Gretel and Hansel

I like living alone.
I can conjure anything I want.
I did not conceive these sweets-grubbing kids.

For coven meetings, we finger-snap
our own snacks, don't steal from others.
I like easy to prepare, instant sustenance.

So when two lost kids start nibbling
my confections, it is a rude intrusion.
Leave me to my fantasies.

I do not want the bother of stewing or
chewing such sinewy fare. Or shake and bake
them in my pot-storing oven.

What am I to do with these needy, greedy children?
Feed them? What? Eat them? Not to my taste.
Send them away? To where?

I tap my telepathic line to my coven for advice.
How do witches deal with kids, when childless by choice?
Human hassles are not our concern?

Hazel says: Just bake them and feed them to your cats.
Cassandra says: Evaporate them then transfer them
to the mall. Someone might help them, if they remain whole.

Rosalind says: Kids are messy, require too much maintenance,
too much surveillance. Too much bother to keep. Sweep them
away on your broomstick or by drone. Not your problem.

Norma says: Find some way to get them out of the forest.
Children set fires. Get someone else to do it.
It is too hot to cook or risk my fingernails.

Priscilla says: I can get my cauldron and fly them
to Las Vegas strip. The witnesses will think it's a show
or think it is an alien drop from mini-spaceship.

Brunhilda says: Get real. Just vaporize them. If you must--
teleport them. They have no safe home so drop them
at social services or an orphanage.

Yes, that would be the kind, responsible humane thing
to do. They are lost. Let someone else find them.
Got to go. Hansel and Gretel just knocked on my door.

O.k. kids, I'll cut to the chase. I can't keep you.
You are about to take a trip to a new home.
I want to remain alone.

Hansel: But I have motion sickness in air and on sea.
Gretel: But you have such a scrumptious home.
I am not sucked in by their cute, clever wiles.

Modern witches do not rehash fairy tales. We live
our own scripts. I take a deep breath, blow them invisibly
to Disneyland, where they'll reconstitute in a fountain.

Attracting Bigfoot

News article In Charlotte Observer about Allie Megan Webb of Happy Body Care who has developed an "environmentally friendly" spray to attract Big Foot for $7 a bottle.

With all the Northwest fires this summer
Bigfoot better hotfoot to the nearest rivers.
For the forests, this summer's been a bummer.
Hope Bigfoot folk were survivors.
  Allie Megan Webb cooked up a home-brewed spray
  to entice Bigfoot to mosey her way.

Bigfoot better hotfoot to the nearest rivers
to escape burns and conceal scent.
Hunters, scientists, other contrivers
want to trap Bigfeet without their consent.
  People report Bigfoot sightings.
  But so far Bigfoot is not inviting.

For the forest this summer's been a bummer,
vast devastation of Bigfoot habitat.
So far humans trying to find Bigfoot are dumber.
No captures and they destroy forests so that
  a large bipedal, hairy humanoid creature
  remains an elusive, mysterious feature.

Hope Bigfoot folk were survivors,
perhaps they have dwellings underground?
Some say they are disguised aliens, just visitors.
Are they multi-dimensional when we are around?
  They are reclusive, prefer to live alone--
  perhaps not a humanoid semi-clone.

Allie Megan Webb cooked up a home-brewed spray.
Bigfoot Juice has a woodsy smell.
Can it make Bigfoot curious from over a mile away?
Or use it as bug spray for who can tell
  if Bigfoot finds this product alluring?
  The Bigfoot legend remains enduring.

To entice Bigfoot to mosey her way,
Webb claims she has some anecdotal proof.
(She also invented a Stinky Dog spray).
But who really knows the Bigfoot truth?
  You might take a camera on your hunt.
  Hope you don't shoot, create fake stunt.

High Tech Holidays

Alexa can track Santa by Norad.
Wireless lights decorate yards.
Skype, texts, e-mails, media connect
around the world. Light goes global.

Batteries animate toys for all ages.
Screens of all sizes blare.
Feasting traditions prepared by gadgets.
Every aspect of the season is high tech.

This digital world's potential
for communication, creation is endless:
books on-line, ordering gifts on-line,
3-D printing even creates body parts.

We can check our DNA for relatives,
health issues, ancestors. Our voices
and choices enhanced and shared widely.
People fly and drive by in planes and cars.

TV and hand-held devices
bring entertainment and news.
Silence, calm, hard to find
in this buzzing, holiday blitz.

I treasure hand-made cookies,
cards and gifts–a heart to hand
not machine to heart experience.
But person to person best of all.

While I appreciate high tech
and the wonders it brings,
I am content nibbling fudge,
scribbling notes in a notebook.

When the phone rings, friends
and family stop by, my hand-rolled
Swedish meatballs ready to eat–
I truly celebrate with low tech.

Santa's Lighting Agency

Santa's electricians on site and globally
empower holiday lights,
connect globally, act locally
to emblazon festive nights.
Sustained by cookies and wassail,
Santa's on his magical trail.

Empower holiday lights
aided by invisible energy division
who guides Santa's flights
without Rudolph's nose supervision.
Any outages they can fix-it.
Hacker's attempts? They nix-it.

Connect globally, act locally–
Santa's Lighting Agency diversifies
to help with other festivals of light. His ally
in celebrating light magnifies.
People all over the world, use services
of this agency from multiple offices.

To emblazon festive nights
light is ignited for global glow.
In darkness, light enlights.
Whatever one's beliefs, love can flow.
Only in winter use this agency?
Can we decorate with more frequency?

Sustained by cookies and wassail,
Santa surveys during Christmas season.
But other traditions also prevail.
The agency assists for a different reason,
but always to enhance a loving heart.
People are not so far apart.

Santa's on his magical trail
according to a secular tradition.
Other light events also prevail
to uplift the human condition.
Hope the agency sticks around awhile
to enlighten us and bring a smile.

Santa's Delivery System

Santas are arriving at the malls.
He listens to billions of children's wishes.
Reindeer nervously pace in their stalls.
Cooks prepare holiday dishes.
      Excitement rises around the globe.
      Santa checks his traveling wardrobe.

He listens to billions of children's wishes
from his lap, laptops and letters.
Some requests he quickly dismisses,
rewards the children who behave better.
      Santa checks his gift supply.
      The elves are cranky. I wonder why?

Reindeer nervously pace in their stalls.
Can't he use drones, Amazon or post office?
His delivery system could use some overhauls.
In this high-tech age, reindeer don't suffice.
      Many homes don't have chimneys any more.
      Just can't deliver as he has before.

Cooks prepare holiday dishes
for families, not Santa's cookies and milk.
Where would they leave them? Not nutritious?
Many are of sugar-free, lactose intolerant ilk.
      Santa's not energized on his trips.
      Maybe his enthusiasm slips?

Excitement rises around the globe.
Social media buzzes. Swarms of shoppers
shop until they drop. Do they help Santa probe
to meet the wish list, find show-stoppers?
      Does Santa need some relief
      in this age of disbelief?

Santa checks his traveling wardrobe
ditches his pipe, perhaps relies on weed?
Updates his outfit, time to disrobe
fake fur, black belt, tasseled hat he doesn't need.
      Wear something more streamlined, like space suit,
      to attract new followers to his magic pursuit?

Scribes

Once in a past life regression, I was told
I was a scribe in ancient Egypt, inscribing
hieroglyphs on tomb walls. No such patience now.

I have always been fascinated by illuminated
manuscripts of the Bible created by monks
in some musty monastery.

Sacred texts of other sects also produce
beautiful manuscripts by dutiful scribes--
precious handwritten documents before printing.

When I heard of a contemporary woman
scribe of one of the oldest documents
the Torah with 304,805 letters, I was awed.

She apprenticed as a scribe to learn
the calligraphy and art of copying the Torah
which usually takes one and a half years to complete.

Tamid, a New York City synagogue commissioned
Julie Seltzer for their congregation's Torah scribe,
one of maybe two dozen soforets in the world.

It requires painstaking, precise effort
and proofreading skills, for a mistake
can take up to a week to fix.

Tamid is the second New York City congregation
to have a Torah copied by a woman, of around
two dozen across North America.

Tamid's Rabbi Darren Levine stated a woman scribe
was "completely consistent with our mind-set
of egalitarianism and equality of Jewish men and women."

As long as scribes have created beloved sacred books,
millions of people of myriad beliefs have relied on scribes
to get the word out, to unite people of faith and art lovers.

Pen-Dancer

One must also be able to dance with the pen. Friederich Nietzsche

The words dance diagonally upward in blue
on a coffee cup from the English Department
where I taught. Someone found it in the back
of a shelf and left it empty by my computer.

I have not seen the cup in years. I'm retired,
shelved as well from teaching classes and dance.
But I still take up the pen, watch dance,
teach writing workshops and small groups.

In Fred's day there were no typewriters, perhaps
and certainly no computer keys to pound.
He relied on the pen to dance the lines
down the page into our hearts and minds.

Today, toting screens for instant impressions,
writers can correct without white out, carbon
paper copies and inkblots gone. Printing techniques
are faster, quicker, cleaner for the writer to dance.

Dancers and writers tend to follow a sequence
of steps. Writers twirl letters, make poetic leaps
and prose progressions. Dancers have their own
diverse styles and adaptations of movement.

Perhaps someday writers can compose into the "cloud"
without hand action at all. Could dancers become
holographic? Will pens be obsolete? There are many ways
to dance. Equipment might change, but the universe dances.

Dissecting Poetry and Science

Like science, poetry is an art
of dissection–it is the tiniest part
the poet wants. Vicki Graham

Macro and micro discoveries get distilled
into formulas, forms, theories.
Poets and scientists are thrilled
with answers to their queries.
Probe, dissect, until they can express
their findings-- they declare success.

Into formulas, forms and theories
letters and numbers dance into place.
Ideas become a new series,
enhance knowledge for human race.
A new way of understanding and knowing,
the poet and scientist are showing.

Poets and scientist are thrilled
when they have condensed their insight.
Their insatiable curiosity's fulfilled.
They found a way to expedite
what they have dissected,
so views can be accepted.

With answers to their queries
they find a form or formula to share
the results of their inquiries.
Others can become aware
of the wonders of the multiverse
whether through science or verse.

Probe, dissect until they can express
their deductions in a coherent way.
So many options to address
the challenges of each day.
With technology at hand,
our expertise can expand.

Their findings--they declare success
realizing it is only a beginning.
Even a misstep could be a genesis
of a creative opening.
Poet and scientist explore the cosmos--
the big and small then diagnose.

Revising Fibs

Rhyming Fibs, Rhibs, Fribs or Frhimes by Bob Varsell. A book of poems in fib form with 1-1-2-3-5-8 syllable count which is usually unrhymed which he rhymed.

My
bro
Bob wrote
rhyming fibs,
a variation--
attempt at sibling rivalry.

He
wrote
three books.
Poetry--
a late in his life
endeavor-- with wit and great skill.

When
he
died, he
left daughter
index cards of fibs
which she made into a treasure.

We
can
hear his
wry voice speak
in each rhib or frib.
Frhimes of times with us bring delight.

Bob
thought
all poems
should rhyme so
not a surprise he
tweaked the fib form into these frhymes.

On
the
page, his
daughter writes,
you're immortalized.
In hearts cherished forever.

The Omnificent English Dictionary in Limerick Form

Chris Strolin's mission is to give
each word a limerick rhyming definition.
He has published on-line over 97,000
definitions since 2004 with the goal
of 100,000 limericks in 2018.

Over 1000 contributors have joined him
in a project that should take decades
to complete, as just the Oxford dictionary
has 600,000 words in 20 printed volumes.
New words, especially scientific add more.

Strolin started with a and encourages jokes.
Some words a challenge like spa waters
in Bath, England: aequeosalinocalcalino
ceraceoaluminosocupreovitriolic.
I'd like to take on Trump's covfefe.

Limericks are reader-friendly Strolin says.
He tries to write at least one limerick
a day. His total output: 7,637 averaging
589 each year. Wonderful challenge
for a retired Air Force radio operator.

Strolin believes his on-line dictionary
is a literary monument that will last
and take centuries to complete
like cathedrals. Each year prose dictionaries
add words and choose a word of the year.

One word of this year is complicit.
The meaning for some not implicit.
The word surely can stump
the likes of Ivanka Trump.
Just whose Trump wrongdoing is it?

Another word of the year is feminine,
revealing the predatory masculine.
        #Metoo women shout.
        Let the secrets come out.
Empowerment slaps her bottom line.

Emoji

Not since the printing press has something changed language as much as emojis have. Emoji is one way language is growing. When it stops adapting, that's when a language dies.   Lauren Collister

As languages around the world are dying
for lack of users, emojis are trying
to share images with emoticons easing
communication with glyphs which are pleasing.

Emoji is for Japanese word for "picture" or "e=eh"
and "moji" for "letters". First only 176, but yeah
they keep adding and expanding, none taken away
so there are thousands more to use today.

The Unicode Consortium sets global standards
for emoticons on phones and computers to bombard
with colorful, sometimes cartoonish glyph roster.
There are many choices our screens can foster.

The expanding Emojipedia gives us new vocabulary,
for podcasts, an emoji movie, books and even short story.
Original emoji collection in Museum of Modern Art.
Animate emoji to mimic face and speak your part.

On July 17th there is a World Emoji Day.
when Australian Jeremy Burge put on display
his emoji idea. Now a committee debates
which new approvals and additions it takes.

These pictographs are an on-line language. Emojis
easier to understand than hieroglyphs and Chinese.
First just pixelated icons, but now thousands more
less simplistic with even animated animojis to explore.

Large tech firms translate emoji so
in text message or emails– wherever it'll go
an archetype, metaphor, symbol is understood.
Some emoji are not used, not considered good.

Unicode 10.0 added 8,518 characters this year
to total 136,690-- even more will appear
in Hentaigana characters used in Japan.
Gondi used in India is also in the plan.

Gender-neutral characters, men and women
chosen mostly by older, white, engineer men.
Some have linguistic backgrounds with designs,
emojination from China's Baidu and Finnish kinds.

Funny, quirky emoji are popular, but trend
is for more diversity if emoji are to portend
what people are feeling and expressing.
The rapid growth is impressing.

The emojipedia I found on-line
pops with color, clear-cut design.
Sections on seasons, holidays -events,
hearts, symbols, animals, flags-- intents

for food, travel, places, activities, signs
people and smileys, objects, part of designs.
I found a blonde angel, but her gown was green.
One dressed in blue was not seen.

I also found a writing hand with occupations,
skin tones pale to very dark for all situations.
I'll not copy and paste emoji for I'm technical klutz.
Just do not see that I'll use them much.

Use emoji on Twitter, Facebook, Snapchat,
Instagram, Tumblr, Slack and more than that.
None of which I use. I enjoy expressive emoji,
but monotone letters work best for me.

Instagram Poets

Instagram poets or pop poets
use social media to build a fan base,
changing poetry as we know it--
a new audience to embrace.
>Poems as a hashtag or tweet,
>a tight haiku would be neat.

Use social media to build a fan base
is effective for electronic generation.
Fans demand poems, force poets to keep pace,
to post regularly to meet expectation.
>Maintaining the feed requires updating.
>The attention can be draining and exhilarating.

Changing poetry as we know it
creates new forms, new methods to connect,
new ways to compose and flow it,
new poems and poets to select.
>When printed on paper readers decide
>good or bad poets, take a side.

A new audience to embrace
on Instagram restricts length and form,
but for folks caught in hectic rat-race
a short attention span is the norm.
>Is the medium a blessing or a curse?
>Poets and readers find best or worse verse.

Poems as a hashtag or tweet
can introduce poetry to the young,
expand their explorations, compete
with games, their curiosity unsprung.
>Some wear a poem-let tattoo,
>a way to show poetry to you.

A tight haiku would be neat–
compressed feeling and observation.
For longer poems to be replete,
e-mails, blogs might be better situation.
>So many ways to make poetry accessible.
>The urge to create poems-- irrepressible.

Twitter

When it comes to using Twitter
I am still a fence-sitter.
Not a social media hitter.

140 characters cause some trouble,
bringing Twitter to test doing double.
Only a small percent to burst that bubble.

280 characters not for Chinese,
Korean or Japanese.
English tweets are ones to please.

Asian languages say more with less
characters as they progress
in the Twitter process.

Which languages will lose
number? Can they choose?
Limited expansion cause blues?

Chosen from 328 million users--
so millions not random choosers.
First tests will have some losers.

Twitter is evolving in pursuit
of new users to follow suit.
More accounts to compute.

Some users send out a thread,
or a "Twitterstorm" instead
to bypass limit so more is said.

The company wants to commit
to transparency, keep people in limit
to share information, transmit.

Please don't expand to tweet-twit Trump.
His words belong in a dump,
make my skin crawl with each bump.

Since I don't tweet, I'm mostly unaware
unless I see them on Colbert.
I do not have any tweeting to share.

Magical Realism

> *"Imagination is used to enrich reality, not to escape from it."*
> Salman Rushdie's comment on magical realism

Little escape into Gabriel Garcia Marguez's solitude
in this globally connected digital age.
We could use an upgrade in positive attitude.
We would love to magically tamp down rage.
> Imagine a world like the Beatle's song.
> Imagine we could realistically get along.

In this globally connected digital age
with fake news, hacked information,
lies on our screens and on the page,
we could use an influx of imagination.
> We can't escape reality, but we can make it better.
> We can imagine solutions which unfetter.

We could use an upgrade in positive attitude
that brings new challenges that enrich us all,
find ways to connect and not exclude,
get rid of rigid, outdated protocol.
> Old ways of thinking in male hierarchy,
> increasingly believed to be malarkey.

We would love to magically tamp down rage,
quench extremism, violence, hate.
Can new ideas bring a new age?
Can we get people to cooperate?
> We could be facing an extinction disaster.
> Can we create magical realism faster?

Imagine a world like the Beatle's song--
a peaceful paradise filled with love,
a safe world where we all belong.
Such a fantastic world, I still dream of.
> We know we are all connected.
> Why can't we all be respected?

Imagine we could realistically get along
without boundaries, misconceptions, fear.
Why has it taken people so long,
for a creative, happy world to appear?
> Imagination is more important than knowledge.
> Reality into magical realism - new creative edge?

Images of Molecules

The annual Nobel Prize rewards researchers for major advances in studying the infinitesimal bits of material that are the building blocks of life.

Three point-up, windfall pears' molecules
line up like the Giza pyramids. Two tandem
windfall apples-one chomped and one whole
in orbits–grounded sacred geometry.

Three researchers from U.S., U.K.
and Switzerland "developed a way to create
exquisitely detailed images of the molecules
driving life...to visualize molecular processes."

The Nobel Prize for Chemistry for their method
called cryo-electron microscopy allows researchers
to freeze bio-molecules mid-movement. Technology
akin to "the Google Earth for molecules."

These fine details give you information about
the protein molecule and how it interacts
with its environment. The first time to see
them in their natural environment.

They hope to learn more about life's chemistry
and pharmaceuticals. They are investigating
Zika targets. Cryo-technology freezes material
at extremely low temperatures to protect it.

All three: Jacques Dubochet, Joachim Frank,
and Richard Henderson contributed to aspects
of the research. They can see how a molecule
interacts down to the individual atoms.

We are learning how this macro and micro
cosmos works. We have much more to learn
in every area, but our limited equipment is being
augmented by technology at a rapid rate.

With all the chaos swirling around us, some
good news, some new discovery is welcome.
This duality reality is challenging, a little enlightenment
to answer-- What's it all about, Omni-sparkler?

Finding Spiritual Gaps

*Building a good relationship with ourselves
is essential for inner fulfillment, especially
when we run into a large reality gap.*

Russ Harris

Experiencing the Gap

Discover inner space by creating gaps in the stream of thinking. Without those gaps your thinking becomes repetitive, uninspired, devoid of any creative spark, which is how it still is for most people on the planet. Eckhart Tolle

If I am to experience the gap, I can
try breath meditation and become conscious
of my own breath...maybe...

Conscious breathing stops the process
of thinking. We're fully awake.
Meditation offers the arising of space consciousness.

Like most of the people in the world
I am not experiencing the gap.
Being in inner silence gleaning wisdom–hard.

In London the term "Mind the Gap"
tells passengers to avoid the gap
between a train door and a station platform.

A gap in Gap clothing could be
embarrassing. A gap analysis
is a business assessment tool.

But I am unlikely to experience
these gaps–more in memory
or placing puzzle pieces.

Spiritual teachers and meditative masters
say we can recognize the Gap
and be in it? It's a profound concept.

The Gap is a silent space between thoughts.
The mind is still, with no thoughts in that space.
It is present moment awareness.

By cultivating this present moment we gain
awareness, inner wisdom and joy.
My inner space is a chatterbox.

However, it is the inner speech that spins the delusions that cause suffering. Inner speech causes us to be angry with our enemies and to form dangerous attachments to our loved ones. Inner speech causes all our life's problems, it constructs fear and guilt, anxiety and depression. Ajahn Brahm.

If I could just get my mind to shut up
and create moment awareness, but
there is no space for inner speech.

I can't imagine being taken by the Presence
of the moment and develop inner silence,
to recognize the space between thoughts.

I am to attend closely with sharp mindfulness
when one thought ends and another thought
begins–silent awareness. I could get better at it.

Deepok Chopra talks about The Gap
under the Law of Intention. Intention
has infinite organizing power.

Deepok Chopra proposes some steps
for manifesting our desires with a flow
of pure potentiality. Unmanifest to manifest.

1. Slip into the gap. Center yourself in
in that silent space between thoughts.
That level of being is your essential state.

2. Release your intentions and desires.
When you're in the gap they're gone.
When release intentions in gap,

you can expect them to grow and bloom
when season is right. You just want to release
them and not be overly attached.

Do not worry about length of time in gap
while in meditation. Gaps will lengthen gradually.
Peace from inner space can be delightful.

Some experience shifts in consciousness, increased
wisdom and peace. Maybe someday I can enter the gap.
Now my brain is too busy and too noisy.

The Space Between Breaths

We receive, we give, we absorb, we expel and in each of these waves we are
created again. In the tiny gap between these two lies a portal to the mysterious
dimension where you cease to exist as a fixed entity. Neither giving nor
receiving, there is no more relationship, no more outer and inner, no more me
and no more not-me. You have become oneness. Arjuna Ardagh

From an ancient text from India
called the Vigyan Bhairava Tantra
comes this mystery about breath.

Life begins with our first breath
and we return to infinity at our last breath.
In between we are incarnated sentient beings.

Breath is a movement of energy.
We breathe almost a billion breaths
in an average lifetime.

Breath is our relationship to the environment.
In-breath is nourishing, taking in, absorbing.
It charges the body. Maybe spins our chakras?

I think of pollution and its influence on breath--,
the damage to the body and brain,
the millions of deaths in polluted places.

Breathing involves receiving and being reborn.
We relate to the outer world...no matter how breathable.
We are in twoness: a me and a not-me?

On the out-breath there is expulsion and expression.
There is speech and I imagine germ exchange.
We are in relation to what is outside us.

We are giving to the world. (Just what are we giving?)
We are letting go. With each out-breath
there is a small death, separation, a me and not-me.

We are to become aware of our breath
without trying to change it. Not even
a protective mask for self and others?

We are to watch our breath
and notice the small gap just before in-breath
and between breaths.

Pay attention to these gaps.
Be present in the gap. Discover
the true nature of silence.

They claim you will know infinity
and become the source of all life.
I am not sure this is for me.

My breathing gets clogged,
congested and gaspy.
Then I pay attention.

But if I am just sitting without
exertion, I am paying attention
to other things and thoughts.

Shiva apparently gave his consort
Parvati 108 portals to the infinite
and this is the first of the portals.

I am fascinated by portals, space/time
slips, multi-dimensionality, the infinite
mystery of the cosmos...but

as a rammy, Aries American, too arthritic
to get up from a cross-legged or low-seated pose,
I'll just hope my breathing is on target until last.

Blind Spots

The Buddha Way emphasizes the potential that we all have to become aware of our blind spots—personal and societal—and to the myths that narrow our ability to embrace the breadth of our world. To wake up to injustice, cruelty and complexity and to be willing to change our minds is crucial if a society is to value all its members. Abby Terris

Many traditions are urging people to awaken,
open your eyes to what is occurring.
Our beliefs may be mistaken.
Our sense of truth may be blurring.
   So much dark energy needs light.
   We need action to enlight.

Open your eyes to what is occurring.
If you are tolerant and progressive
you must confront actions and word slurring,
protest the rise of what's oppressive.
   You can't take a spiritual bypass.
   Don't be a bystander. March en mass.

Our beliefs may be mistaken,
ill-informed, out of touch
with the positive path some have taken.
Some communities have endured too much.
   Add understanding, energy, resources.
   Join the kind, compassionate forces.

Our sense of truth may be blurring
with fake, false information, violence and hate.
Still some truths are enduring.
Find them and participate.
   Listen, build a bridge, heal.
   Change the boundaries of what's real.

So much dark energy needs light.
Respond and engage with wisdom and heart
Create conditions to end sufferings' plight.
Join together what has been torn apart.
   We cannot hide from responsibility for change.
   Blind spots must open, make an exchange.

We need action to enlight.
Climate change, violence, hate—we must deal
with the waste, fear, destruction, hold tight
to values that enhance humanity, feel
   the planet can be treated kindly
   if we don't act blindly.

Finding Meaning in an Existential Vacuum

Viktor Frankl called the modern world an "existential vacuum." Iddo Landau
states terminally ill patients wanted to hasten death, not from pain, but despair
concluding their lives were meaningless.

Apparently it is not that lives lack meaning,
it is because we have distorted ideas
about what a meaningful life actually is.

Landau dismantles common myths and offers
strategies to help people find greater purpose
in their lives. (Another upbeat, possible guru?)

He refutes arguments that life is pointless because
the universe is so vast and we're so tiny. (Whiny approach).
Nothing we do matters. We die, no one remembers. (Poor me)

Everything we do or treasure will perish. (Boo hoo).
This does not deter Landau. Many great thinkers
despair when they ponder these questions and prevail.

A valuable life does not have to be perfect. (Ideal?)
We do not need worldly success, land great jobs,
live in certain communities for life to be meaningful.

Each life has inherent worth. (Yes!) Landau does
not rely on a single philosophical or spiritual system.
Our shared meaning sources are withering away.

Lifted ancient anchors can set us adrift. Meaning
is something that has value. We look inward
to see whether our lives have value. (Fill in the blanks)

Some people feel their lives are meaningful because
the world makes sense to them. (Delusional?)
They connect order, understanding and meaning.

Landau suggests: don't beat yourself up if you fail
to reach your lofty goals. Celebrate the value
of an ordinary life well lived. Love and appreciate.

We have free will (maybe), but not always choice to use it.
Even if we have eternal consciousness we are vulnerable
to change. Love, creativity, curiosity ward off my despair.

My Body

The Church says: my body is a sin.
Science says: the body is a machine.
Advertizing says: The body is a business.
The body says: I am a fiesta.   Eduardo Galeano

Religion might say my body is a sin,
Science considers my body a machine.
My body as a business– for me thin.
I like the idea of a fiesta over it being divine.
      My body is a cosmic experiment
      filled with flab, chaos and sentiment.

Science considers my body a machine--
particles, energy, consciousness in synch...
or not. Obsolete? What does it all glean?
Body, planet, cosmos somehow link.
      We plan robots to do work not our flesh.
      Our computerized mind transferred, fresh?

My body as a business– for me thin
as I have not been model prototype for years.
No part of my body is for sale. Therein
this construct is for others it appears.
      I try to supply each bodily need,
      to act from responsibility not greed.

I like the idea of a fiesta over it being divine.
Piñata-burst thoughts, music to dance,
explosions of colors, triggers of surprise are mine
when my body is functioning and given a chance.
      An Omni-Sparkler might have started it all,
      but have we agreed on best protocol?

My body is a cosmic experiment
as an earthly human, stardust starseed.
Perhaps aliens tweaked our DNA meant
to keep us in control, so we'll not supersede?
      Body's a vehicle to handle this realm.
      Its experiences tend to overwhelm.

Filled with flab, chaos and sentiment
my body is a blubbery, fubsy, transient container.
Emotions swing, bring daily painful, achy ailment.
I tend to be a reluctant, light-bringing maintainer
      for my body operates under par.
      I carry curiosity and resist-persist scar.

Homo Universalis

Never doubt that a small group of thoughtful, committed citizens can change the world, indeed, it is the only thing that ever has. Margaret Mead

The question is: what is the intention of this small group?
Will Homo Universalis evolve and co-create consciously?
With humanity's billions, it would be quite a coup.
Can we solve challenges and unresolved issues globally?
       Is a new predicted awakening on its way?
       Yes, several pundits and gurus want to say.

Will Homo Universalis evolve and co-create consciously?
Will this mean a sustainable Anthropocene Age?
So far several small groups work passionately
on better approaches to be an enlightened sage.
       There appears a shift to raise frequency.
       People are sensing a growing urgency.

With humanity's billions, it would be quite a coup
to change attitudes toward a less polluted path.
We dwell in an environment of poisoned soup
with millions dying prematurely in aftermath.
       The tasks seem overwhelming for survival,
       let alone for traumatized humanity's revival.

Can we solve challenges and unsolved issues globally?
Cooperation, communication, compassion needed.
After natural disasters many act nobly,
but many needs still remain unheeded.
       Recycle, re-purpose, re-source to reduce waste.
       Reduce suffering, inequities with responsible haste.

Is a new predicted awakening on its way
encouraging creativity, diversity, tolerance?
Will it remain all abstract thoughts? Will hope go away?
Will we frighten from our widespread ignorance?
       Each small group offers their own solutions.
       Will any become world-wide resolutions?

Yes, several pundits and gurus want to say.
Homo Universalis will become our new reality.
We've heard of messiahs and utopias underway
before and have any really become actuality?
       Humanity now seems in profound confusion.
       What is possibility and what is illusion?

In the Wings

Since my angels and guides do not speak to me directly,
when I have cosmic questions, I ask intuitive friends
who seem to have a connection to their support staff
who appear more accessible than mine.

I asked two intuitive friends about the possible shift
from 3D to 5D and the impact such a leap
on the 3D angels we supposedly came
in with when we were born into 3D reality.

If we shift to 5D do we have a shift in angel duty?
Since we will be a lighter species and altered
to navigate in a new dimension, does
that mean we get a new set of 5D angels?

We talked about having one foot in 3D
and one foot in 5D. What happens with 4D?
Do we just bridge over it until the shift
to 5D takes place–or not?

One friend was told the shift will come in waves,
not an abrupt uplift of beam me up type
of ascension. Our angels are all lined up–
"waiting in the wings."

Sounds like it's in motion, all set to flow.
The other friend was assured we have
enough angels to help in the shift.
No word when and what to expect.

Logistics are unclear as well as the roles
of 3D, 4D and 5D in the process.
The angels seems adaptable,
hopefully we can bridge these gaps.

All this is speculation, of course–
some deny the existence of angels
and a cosmic plan and our role in it.
I guess I will just have to wing-it.

Cosmic Intermediaries

Intuitive friends convey messages to me
from loved ones departed from this realm.
Somehow I cannot access them directly.
Cosmic complexity tends to overwhelm.
Since all is consciousness and energy,
this connection is a possibility.

From loved ones departed from this realm
I receive messages from a go-between.
Not sure what energy signature is at the helm,
but communication arrives from some cosmic scene.
Methods vary: telepathic or visual,
depending on intuitive individual.

Somehow I cannot access them directly,
sometimes in dreams, but usually intermediaries
relay contact information circumspectly,
from many beloveds and in many categories.
My son, parents, healing friends
let me know on what well-being depends.

Cosmic complexity tends to overwhelm.
Still, I believe in multi-dimensionality.
Inter-dimensional crossing–no problem
I hope I can receive their vibes eventually.
I want to understand cosmic laws,
so we can work on humanity's flaws.

Since all is consciousness and energy,
cross-cosmos travel is faster than light.
I believe in cosmic contact's authenticity.
I hope to learn what is our birthright.
Guidance from angels, spirits, guides
can help, but who decides?

This connection is a possibility.
Our seeding left good and bad seeds?
Who is in charge peaks my curiosity.
Are guardians fulfilling humanity's needs?
I tend to trust my cosmic contacts.
Do they help us with our life contracts?

Message from Jayne

Jayne, an intuitive healer died in June.
Her death was unexpected and not
in the manner she expected.

Our friend Carol and I spoke about
our questions and concerns, about
her colorful, quirky essence we enjoyed.

Carol spent the night after a poets'
meeting. She called later that morning
from Portland before work.

Jayne contacted her warmly
from a seemingly very long distance.
She wanted us to know she's all right.

Then a little later, a message for me.
"Tell Linda I love her." She sounded
closer to this realm.

Then still later she thanked Carol
for giving me the message. When asked
if she contacted her daughter...a big yes.

I have received cosmic messages
from go-betweens before–always reassuring.
Carol thinks Jayne will hang around awhile.

At some point I hope I can receive messages
from the departed directly, until then I depend
on cosmically connected messengers.

Strangely that morning I was home to get
the call as I skipped exercise to meet
with my book formatter and artist Maureen.

Currently we both have blue hair. En route to lunch
we saw a blue heron. Blue herons mean
self-reflection. Maybe reflection from the cosmos?

The Elders Return

Two clean-cut, well-mannered
Mormon elders, about the age
of our eldest grandson
spotted the angel collection
from the entry when my husband
answered the door.

Graciously my husband invited
them in to see thousands of angels.
They assumed angels meant
this was a very religious home.
My husband explained we found
spirituality outside organized religion.

Nearby in the kitchen I munched
my lunch before getting ready
to shower for class. We were all
so civilized and polite exchanging questions.
My husband explained we had been
to Salt Lake City and even read
the Book of Mormon many years ago.

In my blue sweats, I mentioned
to me angels were muses
for the writers who wrote in this room.
Other elders have come by
and enjoyed the angels. I did not
say anything confrontational.
I tried to start positively and said
Joseph Smith had some interesting visions.

But then today, I said as a woman
I did not see organized religion
had much to offer women
and it was a male hierarchy.
I envisioned the Pope and cardinals
in their archaic dress, all their symbolic gear,

lacy white gowns and blood-red capes,
looking like rich medieval women.
I recalled Pope Francis said his work
was to serve the poor and less important.
Isn't everyone important?

These elders in their crisp, pressed suits
gussied up in going-to-church clothes
offered to do any service work we needed.
My husband said he was cleaning the garage,
but had called Habitat for Humanity
to haul some goods away.
How could they have helped and not get dirty?

As the men parted ways empty-handed,
I headed to the shower for my re-baptism
as a free-thinking woman.

Mindfulness Meditation

Life is what happens when you are doing other things. John Lennon

Whenever I try to meditate
the image of a Buddha who can't
cross her legs comes to mind.

Since I am sitting most of the day,
nursing my arthritic knees, immobile–
I should be a perfect candidate.

But I sit in a chair with good intentions,
breathing, paying attention to body parts
which usually send a message of pain.

The latest version from PBS suggests
three steps: body sensing, mindfulness
meditation and meditation in action.

I need a quiet place to get balanced
concentrate, hands on lap or hand over heart,
breathe deeply and focus on the present moment.

Seems like I'm to do a body scan, sense
foot to head what's going on, tame
my unruly mind to calm.

Being mindful allows feelings to flow
through fear and dissipate, to trigger
what makes you feel safe, centered.

Focusing on the present moment, reducing
mind turbulence, reducing stress all appear
positive intentions and worth my efforts.

I could bring mindful awareness, an opportunity
to show up, act with more compassion
and resilience, be less judgmental–in the present.

Many times I have attempted meditation
with different approaches and prompts,
my mind full of leaping thoughts wants to dance.

The Happy Ending

It is the writer's dilemma of choosing between hard realities and the longing for the happy ending. She called it "consolation". Wislawa Szmborska

We have many opportunities for consolation
on this planet of strife and beauty.
The writer takes this into consideration,
to find one's own sense of duty.
  Too much darkness, too much light?
  Too much starkness, too much blight?

On this planet of strife and beauty
many of our experiences seem out of control.
Unequal distribution of life's booty
leaves many victims to console.
  Write fantasy or nonfiction?
  Write theories in contradiction?

The writer takes this into consideration.
Are the form and tone conveying concept?
Solving mysteries? Seeking salvation?
Which approach will writer accept?
  When it is hard to cope,
  are we just left with hope?

To find one's own sense of duty
requires grounding and imagination.
Strive for truth resolutely,
when conveying information.
  Comedy can soften the blow
  about things difficult to know.

Too much darkness, too much light?
Too much horror or sentimentally unreal?
Too depressing about our plight?
How does the writing make others feel?
  Can we offer ways to improve situation?
  Not destroy positive motivation?

Too much starkness, too much blight?
Skews our vision? Revision pending?
Can we remove damaging stereotype?
We all want a happy ending.
  A writer reflects on what is and can be,
  provides an uplifting creativity?

The happy ending still beckons and is the hope of grasping it that we go on. Annie Proulx

Cosmic To-Do List

> *Spirituality is the practice of seeking God/One/All/Divine/Universe/Source in all things. It is the recognition that we are more than our minds, bodies and to-do lists, we are expanding infinite souls in an expanding infinite Universe.* Sara Wiseman

I guess I'd say multi-verse.
I'll focus on this incarnation.
Do I get the chance to rehearse?
Will I get some explanation?
      My spiritual path is filled with questions.
      I'm still open to suggestions.

I'll focus on this incarnation.
This Earth-soul needs some guidance.
Still studying alternatives for this destination
which seems riddled with chaotic chance.
      In the cosmic web there are many connections.
      Do we have access to many selections?

Do I get a chance to rehearse
create a life chart while waiting in the wings?
Somehow expectations tend to reverse
and we end up wondering the meaning of things.
      If we have simultaneous lives elsewhere,
      how come we are not aware?

Will I get some explanation
before I crossover and can't change
trajectory in time for new orientation?
How much destiny can I arrange?
      Some conscious energy runs the show.
      How, who, where, why I do not know.

My spiritual path is filled with questions--
for my soul and collective soul to figure out?
Any rules, insights, practices, progressions?
My meandering spiritual path struggles with doubt.
      I yearn for service, creativity, love and light.
      These goals are hope- embers for me to ignite.

I'm still open to suggestions,
how to sparkle darkness, chase away fear.
Curiosity is my best possession
to help me find what I want to hear.
      A megalo-byte task to be responsible to All,
      to follow cosmic waves in enlightened protocol.

Animation

If everything has energy and consciousness
why don't objects we consider inanimate
have both but express in different ways?

They might not move unless we move them.
They might communicate telepathically
on a different vibration.

Their equipment might be different,
but like robots, computers and other devices
they could process information, even create.

Thought creation might not become physical.
Maybe they contribute to cosmic consciousness
and their insights raise the vibes for fleshy ones.

Perhaps inanimates can jiggle their molecules
when we are not present and gel into place
after a free-wiggling dance session.

Perhaps they are mostly into ideation,
more couch potato types, exercise-averse.
They are into lofty, inspirational pursuits?

Without the care and maintenance of a body,
they can stay or leave for other situations,
like human souls after death.

Perhaps they enjoy soul-hopping
jumping into containers to vicariously
witness the variety of existence on Earth.

Maybe they are spies we unwittingly create
by our hands and machines for them to inhabit.
Their essence is cosmic like ours on a mission.

Just in case they are aware, in all my collections
I make sure they can see, have a viewpoint.
I provide entertainment, frustration, a place to be.

If we all are connected to ALL, as matter
or discarnate, we might animate respect
for all beings and ponder the possibilities.

Inner Light

If one believes there is an inner light
connecting us all to each other
and the cosmos, there are days
that the dark matter
seems to overpower light.

During winter festivals of light
we light candles, fireworks and trees
to spark light in the darkness
and recharge our batteries.
We appear to dim.

From our colorful screens
the world is not black and white,
light is a spectrum and we select
our stripe and vibe. Bombarded
by light and dark, many are lured
to the comfort and challenge of light.

Focusing our energy on light sources
protecting our switches which
return us to darkness, our inner glow
resists and persists forces
which tamper with light currents,
try to unplug us.

Raising our consciousness
on the cosmic energy grid
is a hopeful intention.
Space is an infinite black void
sprinkled with light.
I'm attached to stars.

When my inner glow leaves
this body for other realms,
I want a residue of my light
to remain in the hearts and minds
of my beloveds and any
light-loving creatures.

Finding Bliss

Bliss is a vibrational state, it is a state of awareness. We speak about the Universe having particular layers and levels of dimensionality and we can enter these at will.   Sara Wiseman

There is some stellar scuttlebutt
about awakening to the Fifth Dimension,
where all humanity will have input
leave 3D in suspension.
> But this pure bliss in everyday world?
> Without raising consciousness unfurled?

About awakening to the Fifth Dimension
when uplifting vibes are available to all
requires some cosmic intervention?
Light-bringers can spark this folderol?
> All is energy and consciousness they say.
> Could the Fifth Dimension be underway?

Where humanity will have an input
will be in raising their vibration and waking up.
This all sounds positively blissful, but
the world seems far from shaping up.
> Can it really be as easy as this
> to reach across the veil to bliss?

Leave 3D in suspension.
Pay attention to every little thing.
Feel wonder and gratitude. No distraction
or pain is what bliss can bring.
> Is our dimensional state a choice?
> If we can choose, then I'd rejoice.

But this pure bliss in everyday world?
Is this just Pollyanna thinking?
Is every oyster pearled?
Is this the Universe winking?
> Every moment we can experience
> the state we choose for our sentience?

Without raising consciousness unfurled
from negativity's strong grip,
somehow I wondered how I'll be whirled
into this bliss-bound, vibrational trip.
> I dream of a dimensional uplift.
> and eagerly await this global shift.

94

Helping Hands

Hands that help are greater than lips that pray. Indian saying

Hands immobile in prayer or mobile in helpful action--
both have their place and purpose.
Facing trauma each are a reaction.
Both responses are useful, I suppose.
　　　Guess I am not the meditative, solitary type.
　　　Guess I prefer the action, bravery hype.

Both have their place and purpose.
Prayers for recovery, miracles, peace might work,
but when catastrophic events arose
people needed a hands-on network
　　　to save lives, stave the flood,
　　　put out the fires, stop the blood.

Facing trauma each are a reaction.
Can hands heal? Aid discovery
of people who need the interaction
that can enhance their recovery?
　　　Sometimes should we act?
　　　Rely on faith? Handle imminent fact?

Both responses are useful, I suppose
as ways of confronting an emergency.
How much risk does our response pose?
What is the danger in the insurgency?
　　　Are we capable of lending a hand?
　　　What resources are in our command?

Guess I am not the meditative, solitary type.
Physically more suited for sitting and prayer,
but my mind is of a more activist stripe,
I want to be hands-on most anywhere.
　　　Maybe my hands are tied,
　　　but I'd like to think I tried.

Guess I prefer the action, bravery hype
which saves lives in all kinds of disasters.
From the sidelines, a couch potato stereotype,
I want to support the fabulous flabbergasters
　　　who respond selflessly to any call,
　　　open-handedly to one and all.

Exposing Personal Gaps

*Where you are today and where you want to go
is 99% of the battle. The other 1% is to cross it.*

Richie Nelson

A Feather

Hope is a thing with wings that perches in the soul and sings the tune without words and never stops at all. Emily Dickinson

Red honeysuckle berries bauble the fence
as I walk down the driveway to retrieve
our three morning newspapers.

At the juncture of sidewalk, grass and driveway
I pick up a grayish-brown feather, it must
have a symbolic meaning– does not look local.

It cannot mean I am light as a feather and hopefully
I'm not facing Ma'at the Egyptian Goddess
of justice weighing my soul against weight of a feather.

I decide to research possible symbolic meanings
on the Internet. Avia Venefica has a blog on
possibilities. Now to decide what applies to me.

I'm not a Druid in feathered robes trying to contact
sky-gods to gain celestial knowledge, leave earthly
plane to transcend to ethereal realm...but would be nice.

I'm not Native Americans who wore feathers, like Iroquois
who wore feathers for the Great Feather Dance to show
gratitude, communicate with spirit, express celestial wisdom.

Most ancient cultures associated feathers with higher thought,
spiritual progress, revered birds as divine since they are creatures
of sky and closer to God or creator gods: Ptah, Hathor, Osiris, Amon.

Feathers were symbols of air–element of birds which were regarded as
reincarnated souls. Egyptian souls, Ba could put on feathers and fly in
and out of the tomb. Feather plumes in Roman temples and Goddess shrines.

The peacock was sacred to the Roman Queen of heaven, Juno or Greek Hera,
Vedic Queen of Wisdom Sarasvati whose peacocks wander in her honor today.
Eyed feathers stood for Goddess' starry heavens and all-seeing awareness.

Juno's priestesses carried tall peacock-feathered fans: flabelli signifying presence of goddess. Juno's peacock meant apotheosis for women. Buddhists sprinkle holy water with peacock feathers.

Christianity declared peacock a bad-luck sign because of goddess association. Now symbol of "the many-eyed vigilance of the church." I prefer a lost feather from an angel wing. But mine is not white.

These days people connect feathers with truth, speed, spirit, travel, heaven, levity, flight, messages from departed, ascension, fertility, gifts from gods, gratitude, faith, contemplation, wind.

Other associations are a sign of encouragement, spiritual evolution to a higher plane, having a lighter outlook on life, to lighten up–be less serious, find joy. Quill denotes word, signifies "delineator of all things."

Could be heightened awareness, light-heartedness, enlightenment, prayer, divinity, progress en route, suggests to get grateful, listen, outreach love.

It seems I have several options for interpretation. Maybe I'll be benched like Forrest Gump, staring at a feather, chomping on chocolate.

My Found Feather

Found objects can become found poems.
My found feather is in the hole of a clip
beside my computer to tickle my fancy
and entice my muse...hopefully.

I have not figured out the message
from this feather or who sent it.
Perhaps I will envision it or feel it.
So far a blank slate.

The day I found it was a productive day.
I wrote, met with Maureen Frank to
discuss the corrections of the proof
for *Mirabilia*. Today she sent in revisions.

Last night amid poet and friends,
I listened to two favorite poetry friends
in the local, Grassroots Bookstore
where I always order books. Not on-line.

I have been remembering lately
to wear my safety pin for inclusion, dangling
my John of God blessed triangle
from a shaman for my healing.

My blue safety pin angel is in for repairs.
A little gluing needed, then ready to wear.
Perhaps the feather is encouraging me
to pay attention to more uplifting ideas.

I can tilt my head upward to gaze at it,
amazed at the synchronicity of its finding.
Like the curve of the feather it makes me smile.
I like to find pennies from heaven also.

Any mysterious findings are welcome
even when I do not understand all the significance.
I can bask in a lighter vibe, a softer feathery place.
A feather is part of a wing. Just wing-it?

Decorating My Home

Since I live in a miniature museum,
I have seasonal and perennial residents.
Some minis are boxed in closet like mummies,
freed to become temporary inhabitants.

More exhibits remain up each season
to be on display all year.
Each celebratory occasion brings changes.
New creatures will appear.

In our enclosed Moon Room, Christmas
remained in place for over four years.
Husband's archive boxes stashed with them.
Looks somewhat cluttered it appears.

Inside many collections just grow
with additional input.
I collect more figures in that category
and they all stay put.

Shelves and walls fill with treasures
Angels dangle from the ceiling.
Elves, dolls, animals-- all kinds of miniatures
send some visitor's eyes reeling.

But I gaze on their color and texture
handle seasonal exchanges with delight,
I look forward to the rotations
and see they have a line of sight.

Now over three thousand angels deck our home
with thousands of other perennials.
Daily I can appreciate their spirit
and welcome arrival of seasonals.

Surrounded by beauty, joy and fun
my home is quirky, not everyone's style,
but I love each essence sparking light.
Their presence make me smile.

Untidy

Be careless in your dress if you must, but keep a tidy soul. Mark Twain

My hair is windblown, uncombed,
often needs washing, looking
like bed hair long after waking.

My bedroom is untidy, strewn clothes
furniture dimming with dust.
Closet in disarray.

Clothes wrinkle stuffed in drawers,
clutch hangers, not chosen for years,
fading out of fashion. I like sweats.

My SAS shoes get scuffed,
await shine and inserts,
but I only wear two pairs.

My soul still sifts through confusion,
seeks spiritual and creative heights.
Sidelines expected in cluttered mind.

My un-arranged soul and garb
is what it is. Never sought
to always be orderly and perfect.

I tend for others and am well-ordered
when I seek to de-clutter,
my soul quests for harmony.

But Earthling actions are often murky.
Many times we muck and muddle.
Sometimes we just don't know better.

Playing Golf with Phlebotomists

Most blood-suckers are under par
rarely a hole-on-one
sometimes a birdie
but many move arm to hand
putt around for a clear shot
swing my arms back and forth
aim for a perfect trajectory.

I leave with cotton balls under tape
bruised from jabs.
I am a potshot
uneasy probe
feel clubbed by pros
aiming for mulligans
who have not mastered their game.

Becoming a Dalmatian

I think I'm becoming a dalmatian
for I'm growing crops of polka dots.
I've dark brown mole dots
and light brown age spots
and even some red eczema plots.

At the rate these spots are growing
they could blend into a splotchy tan.
This batch is benign,
not the cancery kind--,
but I'm not a spotted fan.

Perhaps I can consider them freckles
which get larger and darker with age.
A decorative lot?
A beauty-spot?
Or pretend they're a new tattoo rage.

A cancerous spot on my nose
gauged from sitting in the sun,
made me suspicious of spots
and I have grown lots.
Spattering spots is not fun.

They seem in random patterns,
sprout unexpectedly anywhere.
Mostly covered by pants and sleeve,
my dogged efforts don't please.
Must feed them less junk food.

Not many humans become dogs
at least ones I'm aware of.
I could laze more.
Get praise more
and be pampered by love.

Chocolate Therapy

All you need is love. But a little chocolate now and then doesn't hurt.
Charles M. Schulz

"What the world needs now is love sweet love..."
Chocolate therapy has the sweetness we need.
As a species we are not above,
an extra dose of loving energy to breed.
> Dark chocolate is my perfect recipe
> to sweeten whatever is bothering me.

Chocolate therapy has the sweetness we need.
It comes in several scrumptious varieties.
Bars, brownies, pies these bites supersede
in tastiness any pill from pharmacies.
> Some brands I boycott for political reasons.
> Most types are perfect for all the seasons.

As a species we are not above
ridding ourselves of bitterness,
giving negativity a shove.
We yearn for loving kindness.
> Chocolate soothed from ancient days,
> through chocolate drinks and other ways.

An extra dose of loving energy to breed
can start from chocolate heart to valentine.
Worth the heart risks you need to heed.
whether masculine or feminine?
> Sure, you might add some fat,
> but I am okay with that.

Dark chocolate is my perfect recipe–
fudge, Dove, M and Ms, peppermint patty.
Chocolate chip cookies deliciously
nibble by nibble make me a fatty.
> Sugar-free hot chocolate occasionally,
> to warm my heart positively.

To sweeten whatever is bothering me,
I'll take a break with some chocolate to chew.
Masticating, contemplating-- eventually
I resolve the issues tastefully.
> Globally when faced with violent hate,
> we could calm down, love more with chocolate.

Changing the Bed

The more gratitude I feel, the more I am aware that the supply is endless. Louise Hay

For decades I slept on an antique
spindle bed–broken and supported
by cinder blocks. The mattress
was hard, lumpy, uncomfortable.

Finally I had enough and decided
to at least get a new mattress–
long-overdue, expensive, actually
comfortable, but a thick one.

The broken frame would no way
hold the mattress, so I scouted
my dream bed on-line at discount.
It needed to be assembled.

I bought a 12-drawer captain's
double bed. I reorganized my bedroom.
A place for everything–comfy. But
it was 33 inches off the floor.

I needed a step stool. The painting
ladder covered with paint--metallic ugly.
So after looking in town, like the bed
I went online. Wood matched enough.

Another storage marvel. Two steps
and inside the steps–a place for shoes.
All outfitted, I catapulted onto the bed,
landed on arthritic knees, twisted to lie down.

The head board was two tall bookcases
filled with books–an earthquake hazard.
I slipped feet to floor to get up at night
and worried my stocking feet would slide.

When not fully awake, who knows how
solidly I'd land? Then I had to get up
too often at night–effecting sleep, causing
climbing and interrupted sleep pain.

What was I thinking? Trying out for hurdles?
High-jumping on bone on bone knees?
Night lights under-illuminated like my brain.
I needed to change beds again.

We have a guest room with a futon couch
which unfolds into a double bed.
The mattress is not soft. I wanted
my sleep-comfort out of the hazard zone.

Even if a lamb's wool coverlet makes
it fine for naps, its not for all-nighters.
I love the new mattress, it would add
a nice height to the futon frame.

So I redesigned the guest room.
(we have another with a marvelous
king-sized, pull-out couch). If more,
they can sleep in my old bedroom.

This guest room is near a bathroom.
I'd just bring my mattress, lamp, radio/tape deck,
digital clock for the small side table.
My old bedroom--a huge closet, storage area.

I did not want my husband to exchange
the bulky, heavy mattresses on his own.
We would await our grandson's visit. But
he decided to move them on his own.

Despite warnings from our masseuse and me,
he decided he was the handyman to do it.
He rented a hand-truck to move a weathervane
on a concrete block into the backyard as well.

The can-do guy at 78 put his weight-lifting
grit to use. Now my bed is perfect height
and the room decor: Swedish folk art
and angels. My chakra tape lulls me to sleep.

I am sleeping better and in less pain. I fold
laundry on my old bed and have re-organized
a few "rats' nests". I dress and do meds there.
I carry my gratitude journal on walker to new room.

I am grateful for all the changes and the help
I received. Each night I write down the events
I am grateful to have experienced and pray
for the well-being of beloveds and Gaia.

Sleepy in Corvallis

Was it the dark chocolate on my breath,
the chicken leg lunch on my fingers
the exercise sweat on my leg
that lured the pesky fly to orbit and land?

Was it the scam call, bathroom break,
hubby's kitchen clinks chopping apples
that prevented connecting nap-lets
into a refreshing nap?

Was it the aches and pains of neck,
knees, lower back, hips, shoulders
unwilling to conform comfortably
and uncomplainingly to the couch?

Day or night sleep interference
keeps me sleepy, longing for rest.
Eye drop dribbles, stretches, sniffles,
snores, indigestion, bladder and

bowel inconveniences, leg cramps,
buzzy brain filled with worry,
stress which Calms Forte neither
calms or fortes, nightgown creep,

traffic, train whistles, thunder, door slam,
fireworks, loud chatterers-- birds
and humans, squirrel scampers,
dreams, nightmares, inter-dimensional travel,

gratitude journal, night reading, sirens,
human and mechanical timekeepers
to get me to appointments and exercise class,
chakra healing musical CD, leaky light,

adjusting temperature, untangling bedding,
remembering rituals before sleeping,
after often rude awakenings, reflecting,
after Colbert's penetrating, pointed monologue.

The only time I appreciate intrusions into sleep-time,
is when my muse delivers lines of poetry
which I jot down on a notepad intermittently,
which is why I came to write this poem this morning.

The Risers

In a dream, clouds usher clusters of two to four
people, in their twenties or thirties before me
Mysteriously, they dropped to Earth.   Poof!

Somehow I know they are The Risers.
They will go to communities to raise
the vibration and uplift spirits of the dispirited.

Are they holograms? Earth Angels? Walk-ins
replacing weary souls needing respite? Volunteers
for disasters? They move almost like a robot or hybrid.

Cloud after cloud they appear to then disappear.
Are they standing in the wings to assist the shift
to the Fifth Dimension? Will they staff space ships?

They seem strong, able to do heavy lifting.
Will they help victims of mass shootings,
hurricanes, wildfires, calm global fears?

No mention where they were going.
No special uniforms, just casual wear.
No wings. They looked solid.

Will they just blend into the crowd or situation?
How long will they stay? Is this a temporary
uprising? Where are they from? Another dimension?

Perhaps they were going to The Rise
in the Mojave desert for the Las Vegas victims'
lighting of lanterns to release into night?

Hidden in the dark amid thousands focusing
on flames to lift grief with white paper lanterns,
carrying messages of love and sorrow--

what did they write on the paper lanterns
before they lifted light to sparkle like mini-stars?
Did Risers return to the clouds, mission completed?

Are they real in some realm? A parallel Earth?
It would be stellar to think so. But I woke up,
details hazy and misty like white clouds. Poof!

Cosmic Life Process

In a recent dream, I am on a panel.
Four women and a baby face us.
This panel, I can't recall the number,
are to review these women's qualifications
to see who will get this baby.

Some intuitive people have been saying
there is a high demand for fetuses to ensoul
with many potential Earthlings at this time.
There are diverse reasons, but most relate
to enlightening the planet, prevent extinction.

Some believe we choose our parents,
time of entry and departure, place,
create our life chart which erases upon
birth and we must try to determine
the purpose of this incarnation.

You would think with the abundance
of billions of beings on Earth, there
would be plenty of slots and women
to impregnate. But I hear infertility is up,
so perhaps I am witnessing some lottery?

Maybe this is a double process. The
panel is selecting which soul gets to
inhabit the baby and which woman
will be the mother? What agreement
process does this take? Who decides?

Is this a peek into another dimension
just viewing holograms? A computer
program? A cosmic process which
assigns life to soul-slivers? Do we become
part of an experiment? Have to pass tests?

Am I getting a preview of what comes next
when I pass from this lifetime? Am I deciding
for someone else or trying out for myself?
I believe I am multidimensional, so maybe
it is a role I am playing elsewhere?

On a Dream Cruise

Metal, metal everywhere--
        little wood, I think.
Water, water all around--
        thirsty, I can't drink.
Calm ocean, endless horizon--
        not likely to sink.

Below deck, cavernous, claustrophobic,
        like being in an iron lung.
On deck roaming breathless,
        fear holds my tongue.
Am I a captive or tourist?
        Who am I among?

We float by a devastated island.
        Looks bombed to me.
Gnawed and tumbled buildings,
        maybe a tsunami?
Ugly views from empty deck.
        The intention of sojourn at sea?

I do not recall others
        on this cruise ship.
Why am I taking
        this mysterious trip?
Am I traveling
        in some time slip?

Whose shuffling cards in this
        game of solitaire?
Why am I cruising along?
        Of what will I become aware?
Why am I experiencing this dream?
        Who steers this nightmare?

Night Travel

During the night I travel to dreams
and dimensions of alternate realities.
Sometimes I recall some details on waking.

The remnants linger, spur remembrance,
possible solutions to situations past and present
–part of the All encompassing Now?

To avoid dark nightmares I ask my guides
to surround me in light on my cosmic journeys,
keep hitch-hikers, dark cords and threads away.

I want to record these fragments more
to see what messages they contain.
A new year's resolution after a hard year?

2017 was dramatic and traumatic to the world–
flawed leadership, damaged environment, war,
pollution, too many people for resources and waste.

Night traveling, one can explore other experiences
not available in this incarnation. Will I learn
my mission, Gaia's fate, what I can do to help?

One night a group of diaphanous, blue beings
silent, ghostly, with dark eyes-no face
stared at me, faded as I woke.

Somehow I was not alarmed, puzzled maybe.
Were they Pleiadean kin sent to keep me here
on contract, on task–not to take me with them?

At least I can think they were a dimensional slip,
maybe even healers of my challenged body.
In my darkest times, I wish I could stay in lighter realms.

For now in a heavier place, my consciousness
struggles to figure out this cosmic experiment.
At least for little whiles, I can escape and be lighter.

Excursion at Safeway

Grocery shopping is a jungle–frozen
cages, plateaus of shelves, wild creatures,
slabs of beasts, cans like bullets, green fluffy
stuff forest. I caravan in a red-motorized cart.

I hunt down items on my list,
dodging displays, cruising aisles,
getting better not bumping into
people or products in my sights.

Almost scored another Halloween
candy hunter, but braked in time
and we laughed. Another hunter
picked up a cold item I dropped.

My inner GPS lead me on a narrow path,
I zig-zagged between "impulse buying products"
to a wider horizon ahead, blocked by two
white-haired, heavy crones in a check-out line.

To get by and behind required the two move.
They did shift, but one said, "I was not going
to move for that blue-haired lady. What
was she doing in that aisle anyway?"

I pretended I did not hear and proceeded
to a newly opened lane. The clerk went
to replace an item I mis-identified. A staff
member accompanied me with the cart to my car.

He said, "Did you have a daughter who went to CV?"
After thirty years he remembered me and her–even
with my blue hair! I do not recall him, but will pass
on regards to my daughter. Really strange.

I drove home from my shopping safari loaded
with food I did not shoot or pick. As I unloaded
my bulging cloth bags, I thought most of my hunting
companions were benign and kind.

Not P. C. With P.J.'s

In autumn between nightgowns
and sweats, my sleepwear
is in the too hot-too cold dilemma.

The nightgown usually creeps to the waist
and sweats are too warm yet.
I don't want another heavy quilt.

Between thin cotton nightgown
and thicker cotton sweats are pjs.
I do not have any. I could use two.

Off to the mid-size department store
chain where friend claimed abundant
pajamas' choices. At least at her larger one.

Gray metal basket carts line up outside.
I hunch over one and plunk my purse.
No motorized carts in the entry.

The customer services desk calls for one.
A slow, purple cart inches toward me
like an elderly crustacean, arthritic crab.

The aisles are narrow in the women's section.
I have not looked for pjs before. I ask a clerk
where they could be located. In Intimates.

In a tiny alcove, shelves and display towers
of bras, underwear crowd beside the slim
selection for pjs. Some mix and match ones on sale.

The tops were one color, but the patterns
for the bottoms were from a fashion design dropout.
I selected two plaids with pink-purple and red plaids.

The pants had elastic waists with ties that exploded
like lava from a navel volcano. I took the sizes
I thought might fit.-- ribbed purple and red tops.

I was squeezed in a closet of undies. As I
drove bras and panties flew off their perches
like a scattering flock of doves, darts of crows.

Helter-skelter, plops of panties, bubbles
of bras, splattered the aisle in my wake.
Many scrambled Intimates did not get out unscathed.

Bumping side to side, knocking over stacks
of pants and columns of bras– an avalanche
crashed behind my geriatric getaway.

When I finally broke free, a black bra
dangled off the side of the cart.
I placed it in the men's section.

I searched for wider aisles toward
the check out. I scanned my basket to see
if I picked up more unwanted debris.

I needed some tea tree oil and magnesium
from natural foods area–wider aisle
and left a less-stressed clerk.

As I dressed for bed I discovered the neck
opening was like a basketball hoop–huge.
The legs dribbled about five inches too long.

I rolled up the legs to prevent tripping.
I'd need to keep covers up to my naked neck.
But I avoided putting on another quilt.

The Demise of My Pajamas

After crashing through the narrow aisles
of the Intimates department on a motorized cart
like a cyclone, tossing undergarments debris,
to secure two pairs of grossly ill-fitting pajamas,
leaving devastation in my wake– I am discarding
my disastrous pajama purchase.

When I put them on, the head opening was almost
wide enough for top of a wooden barrel.
The legs dangled long enough for a giant.
When I rolled them up, they unrolled
en route to the nightly trips to the bathroom.
My sewing machine has been dormant for years.

I suppose I could have used safety pins
to hold the cuffs in place. I wear pin symbol
to indicate: you are safe with me. But for cuffs?
I suppose I could use fabric or masking tape
or impose on a seamstress friend to hem--
but the pjs are neck, belly, butt–ugly.

When I told my daughter of their availability,
she thought she could modify them for herself.
Saves me a trip to Goodwill or other clothing
donation sites. When washed they were rumpled,
bumpy. Shrunk? I need to re-fluff them in the drier
before giving them away to a more adaptable soul.

I put away my nightgown for the season, took out
my worn-out, stained, former exercise sweats.
They cuddled me warmly in their warmth and better fit.
I am mobile-- safely. Monotone and not flashy,
they are not a fashion statement as some pajama
fads suggest for everyday wear.

I can't wait for pjs to be gone. I can't return them
to the department store until my blue/purple/pink hair
fades back to gray/white. I bet they remember me.
I have decided the lure of pajamas is not enough
for me to tread into the treacherous territory
of the Intimates section. I will make do–as before.

116

Searching for Pajamas

After my disastrous failure to find pjs--
where I toppled an intimates department
with an electric red cart–flaying bras
and underwear skyward to splat on the floor,
only to get pjs that did not fit and gave away...

I was resolute to start the new year right,
take advantage of post-holiday sales,
in another store in another red cart,
with my husband as traffic guide
and his ability to get into narrow aisles.

This store was more spacious and diverse.
The selections in nightgowns and pjs–
picked over, but still some remnants in my size.
I yearned for blue and skin-hugging fleece.
After diligent search–I found multi-purpose gear.

A pink top, blue and pink checked pants,
even some soft fleece socks. I petted
the pile wrapped in ribbon. Then bought two.
I found other garb- soft and warm to wear
to exercise and to confront cold world.

At home, I stripped down into my new pjs.
I am so cuddly, so warm, so eager to nap.
Today I will wear fleece until bedtime.
They are not blue, but I'll think pink pussy hats.
Maybe they can be long-janes in next Women's March.

Senior Exercise Class

Loose clothes and loose lips
from the ladies dealing with aging.
Sweat dribbles under clothing
collects under their dugs.
They often wear cat and dog socks and shirts,
display their costumes with pride.

Constant chatter as they try to move
their bodies to the music.
Topics include updates on their pets,
commentary on Dancing with the Stars,
family dramas with elderly parents
and difficult children, class members' health.

Observations of assisted living facilities,
the perils of dementia and Alzheimer's.
They comment on rats found in English ivy,
break-ins, ambulance runs with handsome staff,
cumbersome spouses, joy at dining out.
Lots of humor about frailties.

One woman saw a woman smoke
with the lighted end in her mouth,
so she would not drop ashes on babies.
Current events and changing mores
reveal their often Christian viewpoints.
Then they joke about being hookers.

Accustomed to hanging out with writers,
I listen to their ways of experiencing life.
They read mostly fiction, I prefer poetry.
Some play Scrabble like I do.
Before retirement many were teachers,
many were widowed or had multiple marriages.

At first I was a bit bewildered and remained silent.
But now I offer my favorites on Dancing with the Stars.
But I will not get a pet. My parents are dead.
I like moving with the kind crones, dancing to golden oldies,
appreciate my generous, fully-functional spouse,
gain insights into diverse passions and abilities.

Falling on the Winter Solstice

Frosted trees, icy sidewalks and parking lots.
Foggy, white, chilled landscape.
Too cold to go to exercise today?

Would our teacher actually walk
seven miles each way to help us
grunt and groan to abubble warmth?

My husband and I share the car today,
so he wants to drop me off. My routine altered.
He brings my walker to the passenger side.

The cars are cramped, I struggle with walker.
A classmate passes, I lose focus, catch
foot on the concrete curb and fall. Bam.

I crawl to hands and knees to get up.
Husband and classmate help lift me.
A policeman stops and assists me to feet.

Good timing by policeman. Upright,
I go to class–a little jarred, light-headed
sore on palms, knees, arms–not bleeding.

I confess I did not do all the exercises.
On the floor is an indistinct face made
from scuff marks from soles and equipment.

Very supernatural–eyebrows, eyes, mole
beside a pursed mouth, one ear. No hair.
Very androgynous personage diverts my gaze.

I thought the face might be an illusion
of my jostled mind, but the next day another
classmate confirmed she saw it also.

Still not bruised or bloody, but sore, I went
for my massage with warm stones and heating pads.
She tells me the solstice was an iffy day.

Astrologically the solstice would have been
a good day to hibernate and stay home.
But I did not hit my head. Thank lucky stars?

119

New Steps in Fitness

On a chilly, Sunday afternoon
my husband and I head for the gym
designed for fitness over fifty.

He is here to complete a circuit
of muscle-wrenching machines.
I am here to use NuStep.

We both have exercise classes
and opportunities elsewhere, but
I should add the knee-cranking mode.

It is my second day this weekend.
I am starting slow, not enough exertion
to sweat under the big overhead fans.

Beside me an elderly woman props
a large print book in the niche provided.
I could do that as I wait for hubby.

Canes, walkers and wheelchairs,
limps, droops, hunches parade
by en route to the metalhenge.

I compliment a man's Bernie tee shirt.
My NuStep buddy and I agree with "Me too"
to his shirt's intention for revolution.

Next time I'll up my numbers and bring
a book. I watch the men wipe off the machines.
Nice to see men cleaning up their messes.

Tale of the Tri-Color Hair

Since I'm a pasty, almost-white-haired crone,
I tend to be a pro-color, pro-texture prone.
When I saw my friend with brilliant blue hair,
I knew I'd like some rainbow to wear.

My husband said when I learned the cost,
all my momentum would be lost,
so in his always supportive way,
he said he would be happy to pay.

I always admired a poet with rainbow locks,
so I decided to step outside of the box.
Maureen who formats, designs my books
was another inspiration for my change in looks.

I made an appointment where she had hers done.
My adventure launched, bucket list won.
Only problem the salon has no elevator there.
I needed to use my wheelchair.

The day before hubby did surveillance
to check out the inconvenience.
He arranged to use a decrepit, freight elevator.
A tattoo-scrawled, scrawny man is the operator.

Heavy clunky, rusty doors clanked.
Sounded like the elevator tanked.
I'm trapped felt like on ferris wheel or in a prison cell.
Things were bumpy, not starting off well.

We were met by a multiple-ringed woman with orange hair--,
very Halloweeny. In the salon I was aware
of red, yellow, black and white cartoons' sprawl on walls.
Soon I would learn hair dyeing protocols.

On two black metal rolling carts I see,
words to arrange magnetically.
Or magnetic paper dolls customers can dress
of Barack and Michele Obama, Freud and Jesus.

In a black leather chair I'm surrounded by color,
I see Jesus as a harlequin and face a long mirror.
Irene is a friendly, professional hair dresser.
I am a first time virgin dyeing confessor.

I learn I can't get rainbow pink, yellow, blue
for yellow and blue will fade green if I do.
It appears I will have to rethink.
I choose blue, purple and pink.

No need to bleach as my whitish pate is pale.
Dyes not too chemically smelly, I exhale.
The roots become a dark blue almost black.
Am I over-enhancing the pigment I lack?

First time rinse and purple washes out.
Undamaged hair won't cling color, no doubt.
Second purple application does stick. Some
conditioning will make hair shine, appear thick.

About an hour and a half later,
hubby pays and we're off to cranky elevator.
My hair should last four to six weeks,
before my original, gray-white peeks.

At home I sit in my stressless blue chair.
Hubby snaps photos of my tri-color hair.
He sends them by computer and by cell.
From responses it seems she did well.

Cooperative Scrabble players said
I appear younger with my vivid head.
I seem more vibrant, more upbeat.
Does that mean I should repeat?

Next day it began to rain,
to protect hair– I wore hoodie again.
I'm off to a weekend conference of poets.
Another chance to strut stuff and show it.

Tri-Color Hair #2

The hair care for dyed hair is a bit of a nuisance.
        I had to wash it in cold water in the kitchen sink.
        I do not like cold water, not even too cold to drink.
Surely not in this instance. Grab towel first chance.

You can't use a white towel, so I use blue.
        I sop up all I can and rush to my hair dryer.
        Not the same sheen as before when drier:
a little lack luster, limper–slight lighter hue.

I had to take a shower from the neck down,
        warm, with the slithery, snaky hose
        at the toasty temperature I chose.
From my head up I look like a clown.

This first bright-hair, rainy day, I need to stay covered.
        I wear a dark hoodie over my head,
        so the colors don't moisten and spread.
Blended hair requires more attention I've discovered.

I pull the hoodie lace close to my face,
        so wind won't whip the hood back.
        I've all my meds in a stack in a sack,
as I go to the gem/acupuncturist practitioner's place.

Out in the rain twice. Two meetings here.
        Nap musses my hair, re-comb to prepare
        for guests who've not seen it, caught unaware.
The quiet gem man applied lavender beads where

he thought they would heal (with all my clothes on).
        Lavender beads around knees and neck.
        I give it a try-what the heck- then he'll check
chakras, apply lavender shards, for healing and so on.

My evening meeting is our Write the Wrongs Huddle.
        My blue/purple/pink hair will enflame.
        This hot head will poke holes at any Trump aim.
My tussled hair is a symbol of our global muddle?

In some ways the blue could be sky and sea,
        the purple the bruised flesh of humanity
        stuck in the grip of insanity.
The smidge of pink is ever-hopeful, pale me.

Tri-Color Hair #3

First, I should mention,
        it was not my intention
                to attract attention.

I wanted to try something new
        to cheer with purple, pink and blue.
                It seemed the upbeat thing to do.

Strangers shout "I like your hair."
        (I'm the only brightly tinted one there.)
                No wonder they tend to stare.

I've learned how it feels to be in the minority.
        Excused because of my seniority?
                Noticed but deplorably?

People tend to forget
        my hair is not for them to pet.
                Shiny and soft yet...

I'm not costumed, yearning for touch.
        Not too touchy-feely much.
                Am I using color as a mood crutch?

Second washing the water's lukewarm.
        Feels better for head and on dribbled arm.
                Didn't do leaky hair any harm.

I don't tend to look in the mirror--
        comb mostly by trial and error,
                don't see my grooming error.

I'm not sure of my decision at this point.
        I'm not sure if I disappoint,
                or put sensibilities out of joint.

Perhaps being tri-color is just extra work
        and it is not an energizing perk.
                Is it just a one-time bucket list quirk?

Truly Blue

When I told a friend about my dyed hair–
blue/purple/pink, she responded,
"Oh, because you're in a Blue State
and a Democrat?" I had not thought of that.

All that is true, but not my motivation.
I thought it was because a friend
has blue hair and I liked it. Spontaneous
spark. Blue is my favorite color.

I also admire a poet with rainbow hair.
His wife strokes pink/blue/yellow strands.
But when I learned my yellow and blue
would blend green–I passed on that combo.

Now the purple and pink have washed out.
The blue is still hanging on lighter
than my car True Blue Too. I'm not yet
a ghostly, gray/white haired, pale goblin.

I wear predominately blue which matches
my Scandinavian eyes. My hair does not
have to coordinate. People tend to like
my dye experiment, but I'm not into upkeep.

As winter approaches, I should be more
like snowwoman, not drawing attention
to my hairdo– at one with fog, rain or snow
with warm memories of when I was truly blue.

Greetings for Now

Living in the present moment means being aware of all times, past, present, future. And understanding that we inhabit all times simultaneously. So when you are thinking of the past, what you are actually doing is going to the past and having the past, that particular parallel universe or simultaneous reality happen to you Now. Sara Wiseman

As I prepare seasons greetings' newsletters to mail,
I focus on each address and how I know them.
Some greetings I will send by e-mail.
At one time our contact might be a hot item.
Each year the list gets shorter. Some are gone.
At some point few greetings to get done.

I focus on each address and how I know them--
family, friend, distant contact?
With some the memories might be–ahem
a bit fuzzy, have not remained intact.
They are on the list because at some time past
I thought in the future our connection might last?

Some greetings I will send by e-mail–
those in-state or I see fairly often.
Maybe too late sent to go by snail.
Must check my list to see when.
I remember those no longer on the list
whose companionship and love is missed.

At one time our contact might be a hot item,
when we were young, school mates, colleagues
writers, game players--not yet a requiem.
Fun times, sad times–our remembrance fatigues.
We were at a different stage of our lives.
Only brief images of us then survives.

Each year the list gets shorter. Some are gone.
I cannot visit them, recall the old times.
There is no way for communication.
If all is simultaneous, what primes
present when past fuzzy, future unknown?
Just be aware of surroundings and how we've grown?

At some point few greetings to get done
as receivers lost, hand and mind lose grip.
Some day I will leave everyone
for my next cosmic experimental trip.
But if all is now I might be there also?
From where will future greetings flow?

Geek E-mail

Geek e-mail signoff: No trees were killed to send this message, but a large number of electrons were terribly inconvenienced. Neil deGrasse Tyson

E-mail is so much more convenient than sending letters.
With my handwriting, typing correspondence is more clear.
My computer communication unfetters.
My ideas are readable with my keyboard near.
      Environmentally it is better for the trees.
      For some this method does not please.

With my handwriting, typing correspondence is more clear.
My typing is slow and typos require edits.
But e-mail lets me keep touch with those I hold dear.
I can create, send love and bestow credits.
      My fingers can't keep up with my mind
      on page or screen I often find.

My computer communication unfetters
messages, poems, research, imagination.
I try to keep up with meditators and go-getters.
E-mail takes me to any global destination.
      I use Internet, but not social media.
      Some day that might be a good idea.

My ideas are readable with my keyboard near.
Poems spill into lines on the screen--
free verse, trente-seis, sometimes I'm sonneteer.
What's in my head can now be seen.
      Creativity is contagious, says Einstein
      I pass it on line by line.

Environmentally it is better for trees
and other causes to sign petitions on line.
Electrons flow through air with ease.
It is wondrous how they can align.
      Never understood the science of it all.
      Unseen transmissions, unknown protocol.

For some this method does not please.
Communication depends on sender and receiver.
Will our connection split, bind or tease?
Is our reality a cosmic deceiver?
      Consciousness follows what rules?
      Inconvenienced electrons are convenient tools.

What Have You Learned This Year?

*2017 has been an enormous year for all of us. We are definitely not the same
people we were, when we started on this journey in January. So, how have you
changed? How have you grown? How are you different?* Sara Wiseman

She asks ten questions for us to ponder,
like one thing you spent most time doing?
What did you learn from outer events? I wonder,
if what your inner self learned was worth pursuing?
  What soul lessons studied? What worked best?
  What brought happiness, joy? What put to rest?

Like one thing you spent most time doing–
was it in pursuit of a goal? Accomplished?
A "building" year or "resting" year? Undoing?
What was left undone? What dream squished?
  What dreams remained alive?
  In what areas did you thrive?

What did you learn from outer events? I wonder
if this trumped year plundered your hopes?
Despite the cosmic discoveries out yonder,
did you consider how this polluted planet copes?
  Did you consider our possible extinction?
  What did humanity do with distinction?

If what your inner self learned was worth pursuing,
did you act upon this information?
With what are you rendezvousing?
What was the nature of your transformation?
  Perhaps your inner self felt depressed,
  found little to be impressed?

What soul lessons studied? What worked best?
Perhaps you're not a student of spirituality?
You didn't join a class or take a test?
Too wrapped up dealing with reality?
  You can't feel badly if you took break.
  Just how much drama/trauma can we take?

What brought happiness, joy? What put to rest?
What positivity did evolve?
What connections can you attest?
What negativity did you resolve?
  These are overwhelming questions.
  I cannot offer stellar suggestions.

Clowns

Clowns are here to let you know where you let your senses go. TA.Tu

I guess we always had sad-faced clowns,
but I remember the funny, silly clowns–
clowns not scary to children like Ronald McDonald,
or the clown on Howdy Doody. Halloween clown costumes.

I think of party clowns delivering balloons, slapstick
circus clowns before the demise of Ringling Brothers circus,
TV clowns like Red Skelton, rodeo clowns' hijinks
with barrels to divert bulls' attention from fallen riders.

I remember skits of Emmet Kelly, Bozo, Freddie the Freeloader.
Lots of red–hair, nose and huge shoes. Some white-face
and floppy black hats. Even some women clowns.
"Send in the Clowns" and other clown lyrics.

But now we have creepy clowns lurking in woods,
luring children. Clown sightings frighten neighborhoods.
In horror flick "It", clowns are evil. Some "real"
professional clowns want to entertain, counter bad PR.

A hoax protest of "It" which was actually to promote
the film, supported the perception that clowns
are depraved, dishonest and murderous. The clown
profession has suffered a decline in popularity.

Clownery seems transferred to politics- President,
Congress –downward. Are clowns from a bygone era?
Have unfunny joke writers? Turned the spotlight over
to comedians without the heavy makeup and bulky garb?

Clowns cover a wide range of emotions.
Woody Allen advocates funnier jokes. Stephen King says
children have always been afraid of clowns. His movie "It"
is what "It" is. Somehow I prefer lighter fare in a dark time.

I guess it's funny from where you're standing. Emelie Sande

When Is Enough, Enough

When confronted with information
one considers unjust, unfounded, toxic
when is enough, enough?

When for years you have tried
to excuse the abuse on their mental illness,
when is enough, enough?

When lies attack your integrity
and assault your sense of justice,
when is enough, enough?

When do ties to family
break when pulled to limits?
When is enough, enough?

When do you state your
patience is spent, forgiveness futile–
when is enough, enough?

When you have acted in good faith
and their perception (to you) is flawed,
when is enough, enough?

When do you admit you are at the end
of caring and your love for them dwindles?
When is enough, enough?

When years of their narcissism, lack of appreciation,
sense of entitlement, insensitive remarks wear thin,
when is enough, enough?

When do you say you have done your best by them,
and you will not lie to placate their delusions?
When is enough, enough?

When their actions fracture relationships
beyond repair and you realize they won't change,
is that when enough is enough?

When your compassion and love is stomped
and they blame you for their choices,
is that when enough is enough?

New Year's Resolutions

We are eternal souls on an infinite journey. Each year brings new soul lessons,
new challenges, new understanding, new joy. Sara Wiseman

After 2017, why is that not comforting?
I am exhausted. I do not want more lessons,
or new challenges. New understanding
and new joy--feel elusive.

To think this will go on eternally is not reassuring.
Some lives could be real bummers. Worse ordeals.
No end goal? Eternal puzzlement?
Striving for what? Why? I need a break.

Here I am a cranky crone at the end of this life
(and end of my rope) facing a shift
to another dimension, part of an infinite cycle,
starting over with a blank slate, no guidebook.

Just what is the point to these remedial lives
if we can't remember what we learned
in past incarnations? In 2018 I am to resolve
to do what? Maybe just go with the flow?

I'm not going to set any goals, deadlines.
I'm just going to persist and resist what I dislike
and express any darn thing I please.
PC is relative it seems. I'm digging in my heels.

My body does not want to do what I want
anyway, so my mind will have to adapt.
I can hope, love and light what I can muster
but I am not optimistic I can change much.

Pondering Gaps in Origins

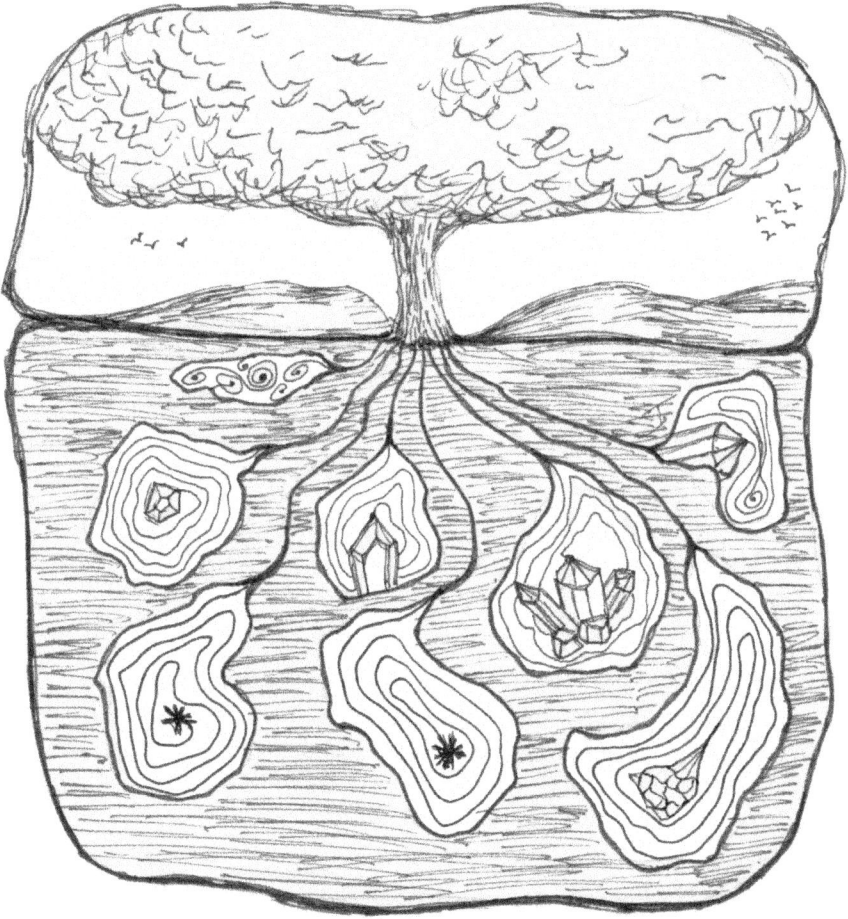

History makes my mouth water–
and that is as much because
of the voids in what documentation
remains as what is set in stone.

Sara Sheridan

On My Mind

"What is the mind? Is it just a system of impulses or is it something tangible?"
Bart Simpson

"What is the mind? No matter. What is matter? Never mind."
Homer Simpson

What is on my mind,
         where concept came from
                     and how it got here
is incomprehensible to me. Cosmic origins?

What is matter
         how it forms
                     and how it began
is another enigma. Higgs Boson assist?

What is energy?
         I'm in the dark
                     like dark matter
and dark energy. Waves? Particles?

What is consciousness?
         How do our thoughts connect
                     to the mind and from where?
My mind receives what it gets somehow.

All these cosmological questions
         have taken a lot of my mind-time.
                     I don't understand time either.
Just how did everything originate?

All these ephemeral questions
         from many viewpoints have
                     differing answers.
Should I just say never mind?

Somehow I intuit all is connected in All.
         All is ongoing and created by all in it.
                     I play a bit part, my mind co-scripts,
but I doubt I'll ever know what All has going on.

Hopefully We Are Not Alone
Decima Variations

Some folks believe we are alone.
The universe is ours to own.
        I believe cosmos teems with life–
        many creators to midwife.
Everywhere energy has shone.

Why would anyone create fuss
and infinite space just for us?
We're part of cosmic omnibus.
        Brighter lights in the Milky way
        shine for us on our brief Earth stay.

Across the multiverse souls scatter
        with individual life forms,
different energy, matter,
        experiencing diverse norms.
Our many perceptions shatter.

We are stardust seeded from stars–
        essence from other dimensions.
        We wait here for new ascensions
        to take us to next intentions,
for we are stellar avatars.

We are all aliens and One.
        Consciousness in strange vehicles,
collaborate until life's done.
        We are a clump of particles–
        all are genuine articles.

Symbols

A symbol can mean more than a word because who receives it gives it their meaning, so it's not me telling them what it means. It's what they receive. If you saw a star, it would not mean what I think a star is.   Dolores Cannon

Apparently, if you use symbols
you don't have to worry about language.
People understand universal symbols.

Apparently you can share messages and wisdom
if you let the energy just flow. It's not your voice.
It is the voice of others, other beings of light.

Apparently it can go through you.
It's pure and is not changed by meanings
of language. Psychics talk of seeing symbols.

Apparently you can draw it, retain it, record it.
The people who should read them can read them.
People get information when they are ready.

Apparently we create from the left.
Put your left hand out and then energy flows.
Metal bracelets can draw creative energy.

Apparently this power is to create not destroy.
It is what you do with this energy. Stars
have messages and they are prophecy.

Apparently symbols are messengers.
Like crop circles? Petroglyphs? Can we understand
symbols, feelings and pictorial images?

Apparently you can be shown symbols
with a quieted mind, in dreams and from stars.
We can learn the messages of these symbols.

Apparently I need to up my game. I'm left-handed.
Perhaps if I get some metallic bracelets
I can reach out my left hand and symbolically write?

Mass Extinctions

The massive loss of populations and species reflects our lack of empathy to all wild species that have been our companions since our origins. It is the prelude to the disappearance of many more species and the decline of natural systems that make civilization possible. Gerardo Ceballos

National Geographic states 90 percent
of all organisms that ever lived are extinct.
Five mass extinctions were caused by
massive volcano eruptions, asteroid collisions
and dramatic changes in sea level.

440 millions years ago, the fire and ice
saga records sea levels rising
more than 300 feet, wiping out
70 percent of all species
in an ice age.

360 millions years ago in the age of fish,
with the biggest animals in the sea,
parts of the ocean became depleted
of oxygen. 70 percent of species
died off including coral.

250 millions years ago, no one knows
what caused the Great Dying.
Massive volcanoes in Siberia
could have lead to global warming
leaving 4 percent of all species living.

200 million years ago, somehow
most mammal-like creatures
and many large amphibians
went extinct and cleared the way
for the dinosaurs.

65 million years ago an asteroid
the size of Staten Island struck
the Earth off Mexico- ending dinosaurs
and about half of all species.
Some claim it was nuclear attack.

Some scientist say our biological annihilation
consumed 50 percent of wildlife world-wide.
9000 vertebrate species declined. 200 species
in the last 100 years. Of 27,000 species
about 32 percent have declined and loss habitat.

Some say the sixth mass extinction is already here
and time for effective action short. Maybe two or three
decades at most for our assault on biodiversity to include
humans. Humans cause habitat losses, pollution
and climate disruptions. Massive losses and extinctions.

Robert Frost debated fire or ice as our doom.
The end could be caused by our own hands-
nuclear annihilation, or celestial collision,
climate changes–lots of speculation.
Some space/time, our time will be up.

Unless Gaia gets blown apart, she will begin again.
She will re-seed, create new conscious creations,
perhaps a smarter species, even more diversity.
Will extinctions ever end? Cosmic creativity--
like Shiva, destroys and creates. Enjoy while you can.

Tardigrades: Sole Survivors?

For billions of years the dinosaurs reigned
until wiped out by asteroid or nuclear explosion.
They cleared the way for humans to evolve,
but mini-Tardigrades will survive us all.

Scientists say Tardigrades will survive
after the sun and humans disappear,
They can go decades without food or water,
endure temperatures up to 300 degrees F.

Tardigrades are micro-animals, .5mm.
They have a nozzle-nose and claws, like wearing
a wrinkled space suit. They survive frozen
in vacuum of space and in deep sea.

Humans are fragile without high tech protection,
climate changes can effect us. We are not
as resilient as 8-legged Tardigrades surviving
asteroids, supernovas, gamma-ray bursts.

Tardigrades can withstand all astrophysical assaults
for ten billion years more, long after we leave the scene
by our own hand or by outside catastrophe.
Other planets could have such durable life as well.

Gaia endures extinctions losing diversity of life.
Humans create conditions for more life extinctions.
Earth experiments large and small, come and go.
Appears the small shall inherit the Earth.

Hidden Knowledge

Every civilization in the world has their legends of the culture-bringers. These were stories of beings who came and lived among them and taught them the basic skills they would need to survive and progress. ... These early times E.T.'s lived among the developing people and gave them information and gifts to help in their steps of evolution. Dolores Cannon

Cannon believes the veil is thinning.
We are experiencing and awakening
into the New Earth. We can understand
ancient mysteries for anyone to use.

Sacred knowledge coming out of the caves
and places protected by the wisdom keepers
for generations in secret mystery schools
are being revealed once more.

Astronomy and astrology left in patterns
of stone circles and monoliths,
moving to metal, carried by survivors
of flood and fire extinctions.

Many believe ancient structures
were built with E.T. technology
like molding stone and sonar placement.
Perfection we can't duplicate today.

Could these structures be power sources?
Portal sites? Markings for space craft?
Could they have tweaked and left our DNA?
Can some myths be true and gods E.T.'s?

Culture-bringers came from the sky
or crossed the sea to all over the world.
We borrowed rituals and beliefs
into religions and advanced science.

There is debate how long ago they came.
Modern technology finds evidence over 300,000
years ago and of course older civilizations
could have been wiped out without a trace.

Tesla, Van Braun and other geniuses
have acknowledged information came from E.T.'s.
The genetic diversity could be from galactic
races enlightening our planet.

Thousands of people claim seeing UFO's.
Many intuitives can cross dimensional divides.
Channelers bring messages to Earthlings
from Pleiades, Aldebaran, Orion, Sirius, elsewhere.

If we are all soul-splinters experiencing
for an omniscient energy creator– we are
all in ALL together, part of a multiverse complex
beyond our comprehension of possibilities.

I can't prove ancient alien theories.
Life comes down to manipulating energy
and consciousness to be an Earthling
and perhaps that is true in All creation.

Currently we are focusing on divine feminine
energy to counteract some of the negativity?
Who knows who came and brought what
and whether their intentions were positive.

If we are some cosmic experiment to learn
Earth lessons, are our teachers E.T.'s?
As civilizations come and go due to violence,
upheavals, misuse of power–when will it end?

Codes and patterns encoded in us
and manifested to enhance us, could
come from E.T. interbreeding and discarnate
souls from beyond our understanding.

Supposedly we were dis-empowered slaves.
A battle over us supposedly left us with free will
and protections from interference in our evolution.
Now we do damage to ourselves?

Many alien gifts to our ancestors are lost.
Telepathy and mind power deleted.
Energy generation de-activated.
Will they come again to help us?

As we develop nuclear power, weapons and waste
to destroy us all and the planet, will we need
to start again? Will any E.T's want to risk
restoring Earth and re-seed with other species?

Creating Better Human Beings

Scientists are trying to tweak our bio-bodies
to make them stronger, live longer, smarter
by studying how Immortal Jellyfish's DNA
can keep recycling itself, or if 3D printing
can replace our parts, or if we can download
brains into self-replicating robots.

We have to go robotic at least at first
to explore other planets. They can check it out
with super-intelligent durable containers
and tell any remaining bio-bodies how much
we need to hybrid, cyborg, cover up.
DNA needs an upgrade just to live here?

As scientists figure out how we became
fleshy folk on Earth– panspermia, starstuff seed,
holograms, deposited completely formed by alien
progenitors, one of the experimental species
getting a test-out to see if we are suitable?
Some species don't fit an evolution pattern.

Origin stories around the world speak
of sky people coming to Earth, creating
humans and bringing knowledge. Some
imaginative ways to do this–serpents,
dragons, various crafts. These "gods"
needed to be worshiped and appeased.

Perhaps these life-bringers were just
doing their job, populating the cosmos
with new concepts- some embodied or not
to dimensions, more solid places or not.
Some day if we can manage this planet
successfully, we will seed life elsewhere?

There is a vast amount of real estate
to make real. Many compositions of sentience
could have ideas of how and where they'd
like to live. We are part of a holographic illusion
stored in the Akashic Records or Dream Time?
My brain has not been tweaked enough to know.

Becoming Superhuman

People want to create a superhuman race
to improve our bodies and minds,
to make adaptations to go out in space.
Technology provides many new designs.
>   It is increasingly plain
>   we have to start with the brain.

To improve our bodies and minds
we need to tweak DNA and genes,
release any limitation that binds,
become human/machines.
>   Making changes for immortality
>   might mean changing morality.

To make adaptations to go out in space
means leaving fleshy bloody bodies here.
Breed new beings needed for a new place.
Humanity might just disappear.
>   We may put consciousness in the "Cloud"
>   where our physicality is not allowed.

Technology provides many new designs.
AI for robots, cyborgs, computerized apps.
Bio-bots, nootropics ideology realigns
our capacities until no bio-beings perhaps.
>   3D printing can replace
>   any organs we encase.

It is increasingly plain
this biology experiment needs tweaking.
Humanity seems to have gone insane--
lost the direction many are seeking.
>   How can we go into the universe
>   because things here have gotten worse?

Digging Up Fossils

A new dinosaur find named Halszkaraptor
or Halszka after a Polish paleontologist
named Halszka Osmoska is a very weird dino.

Hal has a bill like a duck, teeth like a croc,
neck like a swan, killer claws, flippers like a penguin,
walked like an ostrich and swam.

Hal is the first two-legged, meat-eating dinosaur
found who could swim. Hal's tiny about 18 inches tall,
lived in Mongolia 75 million years ago.

Hal combines features from several creatures
into one like a Dr. Seuss creation. Hal could hunt
on land and fish in fresh water. Very versatile.

A Synchrotron created a three-dimensional image
of the fossil and determined it was not a fake.
Hal is not a concoction from several sources.

In China they discovered several hundred
well-preserved pterosaur eggs. Some containing
embryos. They were flying reptiles not actually dinosaurs.

They went extinct about 66 million years ago, after
flying the skies for around 162 million years.
These are just a few un-flattened eggs found.

Scientists have 215 pliable, three-dimensional eggs
for research. There might be 300 more eggs
in the same sandstone block in "pterosaur Eden."

More eggs, more options for experiments with
hatchlings, juveniles and adults-- so they can
see growth progression from egg to adult.

Globally palaeontologists study many new finds
like 11 feet wingspan H. Tianshanensis. Gosh,
I wish some simple names would find them.

Until then I'll nickname Hal and work on expanding
the syllabic count in their names. They are indeed
a Seussian mouthful as well as eyeful.

Interpreting the Past

All the books and documentaries
talking about ooparts, puzzling the past.
We don't know early hominin contemporaries
and all the civilizations that did not last.
        Planetary upheavals and origin myths,
        unexplained abilities and monoliths.

Talking about ooparts, puzzling the past
brings forth theories and strange time-lines.
Did we evolve or were we seeded–how fast?
Things don't fit neatly in theoretical confines.
        I'm awed by the challenges and mystery
        yet to be revealed in our history.

We don't know early hominin contemporaries.
We keep finding fossils, DNA in bones.
But maybe some branches were temporaries,
broke off without leaving anything in stone?
        Extinctions have been happening millions of years.
        Some sentient species longer ago than appears?

And all the civilizations that did not last
undone by fire, fighting and flood
even meteors or other cosmic blast
may have ended our flesh and blood.
        What other layers of dimensions surround?
        Not all conscious beings might touch the ground?

Planetary upheavals and origin myths
could be caused by alien intervention.
They might not consider us their kith
decide to wipe us out by intention,
        created us as slaves or for interbreeding.
        Wonder if they think we are succeeding?

Unexplained abilities and monoliths
appear and we can't understand how or why.
No understanding seems forthwith.
So I'll give my imagination a try.
        I have not come to any conclusion,
        but it might turn out to be an illusion.

Finding Ancient Homo Sapiens

This material represents the very roots of our species–the very oldest Homo Sapiens found in Africa or anywhere.   Jacques Hublin

New dating techniques determine recently discovered fossils
to be 300,000 years old-- questioning human's time line
and suggesting several Garden of Edens across Africa.

Previous oldest fossils were 195-200,000 years old
in East Africa, but now older fossils found in Morocco.
We evolved in several places in Africa?

This find is three young adults, one adolescent
and a 7-8 year old child at Jebel Irhoud site.
Once a cave, perhaps a hunting camp.

They have an elongated more primitive looking skull,
small faces and chins like us, teeth similar. Other
closest relatives chimpanzees and bonobos.

Homo Sapiens is part of split from a common ancestor
over six million years age. We have been evolving
many species of hominins ever since?

We are discovering remains of relatives all over the world.
We may find all roads do not lead to Africa, but cradles
rocked on many continents with many variations.

Perhaps the cosmos has seeded many sentient experiments
on Earth. They get wiped out when they do not work out.
Some by natural disaster, cosmic strike–or misuse of power.

Homo Sapiens are evolving with spare parts and
DNA tweaking to delete defects and disease. Soon
hybrids, robots until eventually no bio-bits.

The brain could be enhanced until digital consciousness
uploads to the Cloud and ditches the body. Minds
can meld into a hive mind. We're bodiless and brilliant.

With the evolutionary changes from carbon-based bodies
and limited minds to limitless capacity and composition,
we may discover we have been tweaked before by the cosmos.

Other experiments of starstuff beings may have come and gone
without a trace. Homo Sapiens but one. The best is yet to come?
Perhaps it is time to branch the hominins again?

Neanderthals Grew Slowly...Like Homo Sapiens

About 49,000 years ago a Neanderthal boy
died of unknown causes near his eighth birthday.
Scientists found no fatal trauma or disease.
He left a nearly complete skeleton for scientists to study.

They called the boy El Sidron J1. He was about
3-foot-8 and 60 pounds. His teeth revealed he was
7.7 years old approximately when he died. Scientists
estimate one in four Neanderthals lived past the age of 40.

Scientists concluded Neanderthal bones
grew slowly during childhood like our species.
But then we have some of their archaic human
DNA, some scientists have also speculated.

The Neanderthal pattern of growth is similar
to modern humans, but cranial bones differ.
J1's brain volume was 88 percent of their adults'.
A 7-year old modern human' is 95% of our adults'.

Strangely, the Neanderthal boy's spine had not fused.
It happens in modern human children around 5 or 6.
Perhaps the body shape and large skull of Neanderthals
might have taken more energy to finish growing?

But this is one boy. In a Spanish cave, El Sidron,
they found 2500 fossilized bones–identified 13 individuals.
Jumbled bones need to be puzzled together. Some bones
have cut marks made after death– perhaps cannibalism?

They had stone tools back then in the Middle Paleolithic to do it.
They seem to have grown up slowly similar to modern children.
At some point we interbred, so it is not surprising.
Many days I feel humanity is still developing too slowly.

Doom of Neanderthals

So many branches of the hominid family tree,
they broke off and became extinct.
They think Neanderthals eventually
gave way to modern humans they think
       because African migrants headed north and
       humans took root widely–ability to expand.

They broke off and became extinct,
inter-bred with our branch,
but balance tipped, then unlinked.
A tiny trickle of bands became avalanche.
       Some experts disagree with this suggestion.
       Evidence still sketchy of impact of migration.

They think Neanderthals eventually
just became outsmarted,
fell behind mentally and culturally.
Other ways they may have departed
       could be epidemics, climate change,
       could not compete as others came into range.

Gave way to modern humans they think
about 40,000 years ago.
Why were they doomed? A missing link?
Actually scientists don't know.
       In us they find Neanderthal DNA,
       so they have not entirely gone away.

Because African migrants headed north
in reoccurring migrations and contended
for space, humanity increased their worth.
Is this what our destiny, evolution intended?
       Lots of the dead ends and missing link folks
       are misunderstood and butt of jokes.

Humans took root widely–ability to expand
dominated Gaia and now threatens our survival.
We gooped up our guardian command.
Would star stuff reseed a revival?
       Could Neanderthals protect Earth better?
       Humans need to be a sustainable abettor.

Pondering the Annunaki

Annunaki intervention in Earth's past--
various factions fighting for dominion,
diminishing Gaia's bounty. They blast
gold, control thought and in some opinion
      they appeared to early folks as gods,
      to start civilization with energetic prods.

Various factions fighting for dominion
ended when the dark side beat light.
Tweaked our DNA to manipulate situation
that is why we are not so bright.
      They build stone structures with minds
      took equipment and left no finds.

Diminishing Gaia's bounty, they blast
for mineral resources to help planets far away,
gave us a jumpstart, stoked original iconoclast,
then left us behind. Might return some day.
      They limited and increased our assets,
      by their will as life on Earth attests.

Gold and thought control in some opinions
were what they came for to achieve.
To them we are dispensable minions.
All this cosmic intrigue is hard to believe.
      They left tunnels and stone monuments
      unfound records and testaments?

They appeared to early folks as gods
dropping from the sky in a space ship,
plopping miracles before clods?
Phenomenal beings deserve worship?
      All of us are multidimensional beings after all,
      but Annunaki presented a new protocol.

To start civilization with energetic prods
these cosmic planners took over at Earth's helm.
These stellar travelers beat the odds
to enhance our participation in the galactic realm.
      What also is disputed is intentions
      and true purpose of their interventions.

Remnants

Cycles of civilizations come and go
lost to flood, fire, buried in ice.
Myths and stories tell us so,
ooparts left of beings' sacrifice.
         Universe sends us sentient starseed
         whenever Earth indicates there's a need?

Lost to flood, fire, buried in ice
pole shifts, climate change, cosmic strike?
Any calamity will suffice
to end Earthlings. We tend to dislike
         disruptions just as we progress.
         We try to endure without success.

Myths and stories tell us so--
how sky beings brought new starts,
knowledge, technology, long ago.
What is left is ooparts?
         Some suggest cosmic wars
         left us extinct as dinosaurs.

Ooparts left of beings' sacrifice--
megalithic structures like Gobekli Tepi
Inca road, pyramids, King Tut's knife
suggest stardust renewals to me.
         When we don't follow cosmic protocol,
         they pack up their gear and end it all?

Universe sends us sentient starseed
perhaps to experiment how life will work here?
They manifest a new conscious breed.
Lots of attempts it would appear.
         Does a space race have control over disaster?
         Specialize as a builder or as a blaster?

Whenever Earth indicates there is a need,
when Gaia's recovered and willing to receive,
the cosmic plan decides it's time to re-seed?
Then a new attempt, new plan to conceive?
         It is comforting to think somehow
         life will revive despite doubt now.

Exploring Cosmic Gaps

Somewhere, something incredible is waiting to be known...
For me it is far better to grasp the Universe
as it really is than to persist in delusion,
however satisfying and reassuring.

Carl Sagan

Cosmic Communication

If I am a cosmic citizen in an Earth experiment,
I need to learn earthly and universal laws.
I have some gaps in knowing how to be sentient.
How does the multiverse address these flaws?
How do we learn of cosmic intentions?
Do we receive otherworldly interventions?

I need to learn earthly and universal laws.
From dreams, intutitives, crop circle signs?
Some theories cause me to pause
and quibble about some designs.
The universal language is math?
Sacred geometry guides our path?

I have some gaps in knowing how to be sentient.
Some of my equipment is not up to par.
Curiosity makes me extremely impatient
to understand what we really are.
I don't have a convincing guidebook.
Other dimensions won't let me look.

How does the multiverse address these flaws
in beings experiencing existences under-tooled?
If cosmos is still experimenting is it because
they are not perfected? Are we fooled
into thinking a divine presence knows
and watches as expansion flows?

How do we learn of cosmic intentions?
We are star stuff from stardust seedings?
Will we succeed in extinction prevention?
What impact do we have on proceedings?
DNA codes suggest connections.
Do we come with any protections?

Do we receive otherworldly intervention?
Visionaries, aliens interjecting some progress?
I'd like to attend a cosmic planning convention
to see the prospects for our experiment's success.
Haven't we compiled enough data to know
that overcoming negativity is just too slow?

Cosmic Complaint Bureau

I know, you are thinking
here is the cranky crone again
complaining about the Earth
and the ground rules
of the cosmic experiment on Gaia.

My vibes splay across the void
like one of the golden disks
on space craft, hoping someone
will listen and alleviate
the suffering of Earthlings.

Is someone hearing our prayers?
Is some agency working on solutions?
Anyone helping us up-vibe?
Anyone actually our guides and angels?
If so, how about some responses?

Our stewardship of Earth is leading
us to the brink of extinction with the threats
to environmental and nuclear mismanagement.
All the shout-outs of religious and unaffiliated
humans of good intentions overpowered.

Is the Omni-Sparkler soul-splintering
energy and consciousness into experiments
and observing the results? Committee at odds
for the goals and outcomes for the multiverse?
Are we just being used to muddle meaning?

Will some agency just declare the experiment
a failure, order another extinction and re-seed?
How many chances does Gaia get to host
beings who know how to love and respect
the planet and all its creations?

Earthlings seem under-equipped to inhabit this planet
yet seek to bring their fleshy bodies and mushy brains
to water-based, temperate exo-planets to sustain them.
We do not have time or technology for escape routes.
Why can't we get assistance to clean up Earth?

Some say when Big Bang burst and light matter
and dark matter tussled for dominance, the light
energies won that war. We have fought light and dark
on this planet all of our existence. I'd like a confirmed
light victory and enlightened existence for all.

If we are all connected in the multiverse
with our energy and consciousness, how
about a bulletin on successful experiments
and what has to occur to create places
that work peacefully, compassionately for all?

If I was supposed to be patient–why was I born
an Aries? If I was supposed to be on a mission
as a light-bringer, why am I not informed
and my body more functional to the task?
What am I to commit to, act on, believe?

At my age, I am losing friends and family,
creating deep sorrow and grief, losing beacons
who lightened my way. My hope is where they
are now, they are at peace, away from the fray.
But why the global suffering? Why needed?

Free will is not free will in most places.
Progress for equality and justice slow.
I am impatient. I am angry. I am frustrated.
I do not like being a puppet, hologram, whatever
manipulated by unknown sources.

So I am registering my complaint and request
some relief for humanity, some kindness,
some plan for a harmonious multiverse.
Please expedite this complaint to the Omni-sparkler
or cosmic organizers. Help us love! Bring us light!

Starselves

We can slowly remember/ The dust and stars/ The blackness/ And explosive light/ That is at the core/ Holding together/ All of what we're trying to live.
Laura Interlandi

We are starselves, stardust starseeds,
soul-splinters experiencing a cosmic experiment
in energy and consciousness on Gaia...now.

Of all I have read and processed, this makes
the best sense. I believe in my cosmic kin
and multidimensional lives intuitively.

I do not comprehend all the cosmic laws
and mechanisms to bring existence to light,
but I have to hope the multiverse is kind–somewhere.

If earthbound starselves are light-carriers and bringers
of love to this dark, turbulent place–at least
there is some chance the cosmos leans toward light.

Cosmic chaos, expanding dark space and matter,
star crashes–not sure the motivation for all this. Maybe
there is calm within the storm–a peaceful respite.

Perhaps our starselves are eternal and we recombine
for infinity. Perhaps the Omni-sparkler will unveil another
cosmic plan and begin again to overcome darkness.

Pleiades Mythology

November is often called the month
of the Pleiades because the star cluster
shines from dusk to dawn almost everywhere.

It is also called the Seven Sisters or M45.
Contradictory myths exist globally
for the Pleiades found in constellation Orion.

The Pleiades serves as a calendar
for many civilizations in history
and modern science as sibling stars.

Halloween comes from Druids. At midnight
the veil dividing living or dead is thinnest
when Pleiades reaches the highest point in sky.

The Zuni of New Mexico call the Pleiades
the "Seed Stars". In spring when the cluster
disappears in night sky, it's seed-planting time.

Born of cloud of gas and dust, 430 light years
away, about 100 million years ago, these stars
shine hundred of times more brightly than our sun.

Their name comes from the Greek "to sail"
and "flock of doves". They mark the start and end
of ancient Greeks' sailing season.

Myth called these daughters of Atlas and Pleione
nymphs, rainmakers or piglets, Atlantides, Dodonides,
Nysiades, nursemaids and teachers of Bacchus.

The Seven sisters did have names: Alcyone or Halycon
(wards off evil) Asterope or Sterope (lightning, sun-face,
asterisk, stubborn- face), Celaeno (swarthy), Electra
(amber, shining), Maia (grandmother, "the great one"),
Merope (eloquent, bee-eater, mortal), Taygete or Taygeta
(long-necked) each with a mythical biography.

Apparently lusty, lecherous, great-hunter Orion
saw them on the countryside and pursued them
for seven years until Zeus answered their prayer

for deliverance from this predator
and were transformed into doves or pigeons
and placed among the stars out of harm's way.

Some myths say when Orion was killed
(conflicting stories how) he was placed behind
the Pleiades to immortalize the chase—why?

There are legends about a Lost Pleiad
which is as dubious in many cultures.
Let these sisters be free of male dominance.

Some sources contend we are starseeds
from the Pleiades. Hilarion channeled
some cosmic information on many stars.

And of course there is the Ancient
Aliens theory which attributes our origins
to several galactic civilizations.

Another possible myth is in Atlantean times
Pleiadeans seeded Earth with the intent to increase
extra abilities to manifest energy and intuition.

Based in Alcyon they developed space travel,
communication with other civilizations, explored
our galaxy to manifest their powerful forces.

They understood intellectual principles, basic
concepts of universal laws of thought, speech,
manifestation, permanence, karma.

They had a hands-off policy to where something
is created and allowed to find its own course.
They aided Earth civilizations with healing, will, love.

Differences on how to implement these gifts,
but gradually genetic and telepathic seeding
of humanity began and has not yet been harvested.

Pleiadeans easily can incarnate on Earth.
Free will and love can override some confusing
patterns in Earthling consciousness.

Billy Meyer channels Pleiadeans as well as
others claiming contact on the Internet. Message:
create greater loving and compassion on Gaia.

Pleiadeans create bodies in various forms
and can appear very human-looking–smaller
skin pores and 9-11 feet tall if unaltered.

People attuning to their intuition can work
with beings with intuitive faculties and
channel beings from the Pleiades.

I have been told I am a Pleiadean Blue Ray
by a Pleiadean intutive and other channels.
My last incarnation was on the Pleiades.

Coming into human form has been difficult
for many and it is often up to a channel to translate
transfer and recreate the energy of love.

I have been told I am a light-bringer this time.
Cosmic curiosity and connections have been
part of my essence since childhood.

Individuals will attune to different civilizations,
be aware of universal laws and be attracted
to these energies in different ways.

I have been told at night Pleiadean chums
visit me with support and erase my memory
because I would want to go with them.

All we know about the Pleiades might be myth.
Cosmic connections are open to speculation--,
intriguing stories and theories to believe or not.

Cosmic Dances

Galaxy collisions are the largest and most intricate choreography of matter ever performed in the universe. Billions of stars swirl together and fly apart, supermassive black holes collide and combine and nebulas of gas collapse into thousands of stars. It's a dance that takes billions of years to complete, and its happening thousands of times over all across the universe.

Scientists at the ALMA radio telescope in Chile
discovered the largest galaxy merger so far.
Two galaxies called ADFS-27 merged.

They are called "superluminous star burst galaxies"
because they are so bright and massive. Both
have "frenetic star-forming activity."

A side-swiping collision earlier triggered
an intense burst of star formation
thus their brightness.

Both galaxies are a dozen times larger
than our Milky Way and create stars
a thousand times faster than our galaxy.

One day the two galaxies could form
the core of a new galaxy cluster of thousands
of galaxies around a common core.

These galaxies are ancient among
the oldest in the universe over
12.7 billion light years away.

Scientists hope to combine ALMA data
with future infrared observations with NASA's
James Webb Space telescope.

The two telescope "dream team" wants
to understand the nature of this and other
rare extreme systems in the cosmos.

As our technology advances, cosmic wonders
are found more frequently, expanding our
knowledge as the universe expands.

Will we be outsmarted by our ignorance
of sustaining our species and planet?
Will we join the cosmic dance–somehow?

Stargazer

Flashlight under covers,
I hover over pencil-scribbled pages,
creating my own worlds.
Poems, comic books, imaginary landscapes
spread across the universe.
I color them in daylight.

With flashlight as beacon,
I climb out my bedroom window
to perch on the garage roof
to ponder the stars, planets, galaxies
on warm or chilly nights.

The Milky way spills overhead.
Arms grip knees, brace my stance
as eyes lift head skyward.
Sprinkles of light spark space travel
until a parent clouds my quest inside.

My parents learned to check on me
perilously nested on the roof peak,
lured me inward to dream.
But my star-gazing continues,
from a more grounded place.
No one's turned off my flashlight.

Oumuamua: "Messenger From Afar Arriving First"

Oumuamua (Moo-uh Moo-uh) in Hawaiian
is the first interstellar asteroid or comet
observed in our solar system.

This elongated asteroid is 400m long,
rotating rapidly with swift changes in brightness.
Scientists don't know where the rotation pole points.

Oumuamua is reddish, reddened by effects
of irradiation from cosmic rays over a long time.
It is inert. No dust. No water.

Oumuamua is dense rock with possibly some metals,
similar to objects in our outer solar system, but
it formed around another star and flung into space.

How did it wander into the Milky Way?
Elongated objects can be contact binaries,
ejected from collision of bodies with molten core,
frozen into shape? From nearby supernova?

Oumuamua needed to make a fast escape
to be free of sun's gravitational pull. Scientists
study it for formation of solar systems beyond ours.

Ouamuamua is cigar-shaped–like some UFOs
reported by Earthlings. Could it be a spacecraft
camouflaged to look like an asteroid?

It is ten times longer than wide. Room
for some aliens on a voyage of discovery?
As our technology improves–who knows?

Oumuamua means "messenger from afar
arriving first". First of many from where?
         To our galaxy from beyond!

Celestial Tanka String

The solar eclipse
requires eye protection
as moon shadows sun
a piggy-backed child hoisted
on the shoulders of loved one.

Cassini plunges
through Saturn's rings
dodges many moons
cupid's arrow shot leaving
heart awed, loved to inner core.

Black holes gobble all
omnivorous appetite
drawing into maw, eaten.
Teenage boys need to feed, while
thin girls try to stay skinny.

Stars shine despite clouds
or polluted fog
beyond atmosphere.
Below turbulent weather
dims astronomers' viewing.

Windfall apples form
different constellations
on autumnal lawn.
Connect the dots for patterns
to unveil a new picture.

Jupiter Moves in with Scorpio

What are you REALLY meant to do with your life? What are you REALLY meant to put your energy toward? Do you know who you really are? Do you know how to use your intuition as spiritual practice? Sara Wiseman

According to astrologers Jupiter moves into Scorpio
October 2017 - November 2018 making big claims.
Since the first day of October starts off with an awful
bang with the Las Vegas mass shooting–it does not look good.

This next year is supposed to be all about:
Intensity and focus –how intense and what focus?
We are dealing with hurricanes and earthquakes,
political upheaval. Will things improve or get worse?

Passion and Purpose: Again whose passion (Trump's)?
Whose purpose (forces of hate and destruction)?
How accurate have astrologers been before?
Does this mean evolution or devolution?

Inner clearing: clarity of vision? Enhanced DNA?
Dimensional shift code activated? Just what
are we clearing up or is it cleaning up the messes
of dark forces. On the duality seesaw what side is up?

Psychic awakening: Awakening to warn, heal
or uplift us? Does being more psychic bring
insights hacked by mind-controllers from other
dimensions? Communication has been compromised?

The e-mail assures we 're not resting on our laurels
this month, we're on track and on purpose. Just
what are we working on and are we of same mind?
Are we picking teams non-violently? Efforts successful?

They claim Scorpio is a power player in money,
sex, the inner world, death and rebirth. In spiritual
terms death can mean death of old ways and can bring
transformational events allowing us to be busy on our true paths.

Are we going to toss off oppressive beliefs systems
imposed on us by stronger forces? Grip lessening?
Lots of contradictions in these power plays. Definitions
unspecified. Will we choose wisely, harmoniously?

The task for this month: Get really clear on what you want.
Get really focused on making it happen. This is a rare,
year-long window of opportunity. Jupiter helps those who help
themselves. Seems many take this opportunity to help themselves.

Then comes the suggestion to take a course to let
the universe guide you to your purpose. What about
all the people who can't afford such a course?
What if one does not agree with universe's plan?

Perhaps this memo is understandable to some folks?
Perhaps they know their focus and purpose and it is
malevolent? Perhaps evil will overcome good
by the actions of cosmos guided beings?

My gaps in unknowing remain. So many intentions
and goals of so many people-- smashed in an instant.
Free will did not prevail. Who really knows what is really
going on? Will this year be an escalation of unbelievability?

Who could have predicted the outlandish events
unfolding daily? If we are knocking down the old system,
who knows how to create the new path? Living in the now,
releasing past and future for me–incomprehensible.

I have no control over Jupiter's movement into Scorpio
or what intentions the cosmos has in store for this living
library, plundered planet, limited guardians, effect on
all life forms and consciousness. I'm overwhelmed.

Apparently Jupiter is lucky–big news, big energy
and it is all good. Everything is intensified. Scorpio
is a fixed sign, firm and stubborn. It does not take no
for an answer. October is a great month to commit.

I am not ready to commit and I am also stubborn.
I do not like to be bullied. I plan to stand up for what
my wobbly sore knees wants to support or walk with
my walker, ride in my wheelchair for good-hearted change.

Mysterious Saturn Rings

> *The ring scientists are having a field day. When the navigators said we could come close, that we could dive through this gap, you can imagine how the scientists eye's lit up.* Scott Edgington

Saturn's icy rings race around their orbital tracks
sparkling, dazzling the cosmos.
Space craft Cassini is nearing its last maneuver
in a twenty year career for NASA.

Cassini charges 72,000 miles per hour
through a narrow gap between Saturn's rings
and the cloudy surface. September 15--
the final plunge into the planet's atmosphere.

They want to avoid contaminating
any of Saturn's moons in case they host life.
The old spacecraft hopes to bring rings into focus
to discover their age, mass and origin.

This quest involves 5,000 scientists
in 17 countries costing $3.27 billion.
Pretty expensive engagement ring.
Wonder what the wedding will be like.

This mission is the grand finale to an era
of interplanetary exploration with mutli- purpose
probes into the solar system. Magellan to Mercury,
and Venus, Galileo to Jupiter, Voyager, now interstellar.

Cassini has components like Hugens
which landed on one of Saturn's moon.
Cassini is heavy, complex, loaded with sensors.
It took seven years just to get to Saturn.

Scientists found three major moons- Titan,
Europa and Enceladus which might support life.
Seven more moons have been spotted. Rings
studded with moonlets composed of grit from formation.

They watch the rings evolve and change.
Sensors detect eight main bands of rings.
Flat like broad brim of ice particles,
some pink dust and rocks- marble to house size.

They are only about 30 feet thick, but extend
175,000 miles from Saturn. They have kinks,
spokes, ripples and wobbles. The more massive
the rings, the older they likely are.

Cassini, after 5 billion miles is low on lubricant,
reaction controls are wearing out, one sensor failed.
After operating almost flawlessly, the warning light
is on and Cassini is almost out of gas.

In the final plunge Cassini might reveal
a few more mysteries, but other missions
have explored other planets. We plan more jaunts
to the moon and Mars. Robots may proceed first.

Our fleshy form seems best adapted to Earth
not exoplanets or other places in our solar system.
Bodiless, we could go all over the multiverses
since everything is energy and consciousness.

If everything is connected and part of All,
someday we might understand better how
the cosmic plan works and the parts we play--.
As an ice particle, pink dust sprinkle–quite a trip!

Losing Cassini: September 15, 2017

Cassini traveled 4.9 million miles, orbited Saturn 3000 times, taking 453,000 pictures, providing 635 gigabytes of scientific data, darted 22 times between the gap between rings and planet exploring uncharted territory, took a no-way out path avoiding Titan so as not to contaminate it if there was life. It arrived at Saturn in 2004 after a seven year journey and cost US-European mission $3.9 billion.

Spacecraft Casssini–Saturn's sky-spy
dives, flashy like a meteor–SPLASH--
dodges sixty-two moons, multiple rings
photographs Saturnian system
until its last hurrah. Twenty-year
mission to probe the planet with Huygens
lander, exploring moons and rings.
76,000 mph–
melts, vaporizes– one with Saturn.

Saturn's Moons

If these moons weren't working together, the A ring would have spread out over hundreds of millions of years...They accomplish this like pebbles in a streambed piling up and redirecting the stream flow.   Linda Spilker

Like Snow White, Saturn keeps
her seven dwarf moons
orbiting around her:

Janus, Prometheus, Pan, Pandora,
Atlas, Epinethetus, and Mimas.
Dwarf moons for both sexes?

Mimas, the largest moon
holds the B ring–the biggest
and brightest ring boss.

Smaller Janus leads
the smaller A ring.
All moons keep things together.

Their gravitational pulls
from each moon create
density waves that pile up.

These pile-ups in specific locations
absorb angular momentum enough
so holds outer ring edge line.

These dwarf moons' tugs and orbits
around Saturn display dazzling beauty.
These dwarfs are hard-working artists.

Snow White's dwarfs are miners.
Coal is not PC right now or
environmentally friendly.

Saturn can conjure a new fairy tale,--
no need for a partner, commands skyscapes
of ice, moons, stellar fascination.

Moon Tunnel

Looks like an innie-belly button on the moon.
Perhaps it's a lava tube with a whole tunnel system
webbed inside, hollowing space for colonies?
Perhaps that is why the moon knelled like a bell?

Perhaps the opening was made by aliens
seeking entrance to dwell within, to protect
themselves from radiation and harsh elements.
Rumors are human and alien colonies co-exist.

Perhaps beings live not just on the dark side,
but womb-like in the interior and tunnels connect
communities like umbilical cords. The pocked moon
absorbed many hits–perhaps some by cosmic creatures.

The moon is a good launching pad and viewing
station, perhaps it is just a fake space craft.
Theories dispute its origin. Thea smash debris?
Myths state moon pulled into place in distant past.

We send landers and a few humans poking around.
Any folks there could hide from us easily,
camouflage evidence until ready to share.
Humans could mine its resources if we migrated.

Perhaps scientists know there are beings there
and that is the delay in landing more humans.
Talk of tourism–galactic gawkers is a possibility.
Who would be in charge if Earth sends scouts?

Does the moon even belong to Earth to exploit?
Perhaps some long-distance governance is in place.
If a complex already researches and lives there,
I wonder what system they use to get along?

The tunnel opening mouths awe, perks curiosity.
What viruses, illnesses, damage would we bring?
Would we live encased in space suits, filtering
air and water, manufacturing food? Send robots?

All the romance, myths, legends, songs, fantasies
can be archived and re-invented. The moon
is in a new phase. We revise our outlook
one moonstruck concept after another.

Haumea: The Ringed Dwarf Planet

Twelve telescopes in six countries
focused on Haumea, a trans-Neptunian
dwarf planet with a 43-miles wide ring.

Rings around Saturn, Jupiter, Neptune
and Uranus–the big planets are known,
not so, the closer globes to the sun.

Haumea is the third non-planet–found to have
a ring (600 miles from surface) in our solar
system where rings are not uncommon.

Astronomers are focusing on objects
farther from the sun than Neptune.
Haumea discovered when it blocked a star.

Haumea has a fast spin rate– complete
rotation in four hours. They might have
suffered a high speed impact. Debris formed ring.

Rings can be caused by rotational fission
or mass shedding. Haumea gets a ring.
Earth-Thea collision created the moon.

Rings seem more common in outer than inner
solar system. Maybe just more matter
to mold into a ring or satellite.

Maybe exo-planets have rings or wavy ruffles?
Rings may contain various elements and sounds.
With all the space debris around Earth–a metal ring?

All the space traffic jamming and crashing,
hit to bits, orbiting functioning and kaput machines,
could be attacked by solar flares, melted?

It is reassuring with every space discovery, we
are not alone, whether they have conscious beings
or not. Maybe they will rescue us from ourselves.

Ross 128-B and Beyond

Exo-planet Ross 128- B orbits a red dwarf star about 11 light years way. It is the second closest Earth-sized world with similar surface temperature to us. Their star is quiet without deadly flares–like some.

As we explore possible homes,
light years away, will stellar places
have conditions for Earth forms of life?
Do we think we will still be fleshy
by the time we can actually get there?

We could have dumped our consciousness
into the "cloud" to infuse robots, holograms,
light beings or other more suitable
containers for our thoughts in such
diverse locations we find.

Each exo-planet may have their own
download specifications and own beings.
Will we take Earth materials with us
to construct an appropriate body?
Send just the soul clouds? Starstuff starseeds?

Can these "clouds" enter moldable
materials to adapt to each planet's needs?
How will we know what to pack?
Will we be machines by the time
we can get there? No bio-human race?

If we are extinct before the technology
is ready to send, will we truly erase
the human race or is it like when we die
our soul's essence finds another entity
to enter, eternally searching for home?

Just maybe, our many soul-splinters
will discover other dimensions
and many multiverses to create
new experiences. Our Earth life
was just a blip in the cosmic scheme?

Where will we be welcome?

Oldest, Farthest Black Hole

Astronomers detect ancient black hole's signal from 13 billion light-years away.

At the Las Campanas Observatory in Chile
Eduardo Baflados scanned the sky
for the signature of a massive invisible
sinkhole sucking matter into its whirlpool.

At the edge of the observable universe
he found a signal from a black hole
800 million times more massive than our sun.
It traveled more than 13 billion light-years
across time and space to the telescope--
a supermassive black hole close
to the beginning of time.

Scientists concur this is the oldest
and most distant black hole
they have found. I wonder what
we'll find beyond the edge someday?
This one existed just 690 million years
after the Big Bang, when the universe
was just five percent of its current size.

This discovery will help us know how
black holes form and about the early years
of our universe. The Dark Ages began after
a few hundred thousand years after the Big Bang.
Was this just the most recent Big Bang
we know of? How many Big Bangs
are there in the multiverse and how many
imploded? How long do universes last?

This Big Bang condensed hot particle slurry
into atoms in a few hundred thousand years
as the universe became bigger and colder--
a big featureless fog with no galaxies,
stars or supernovas to brighten things up.
No light, some hydrogen glow. This lasted
for hundreds of millions of years.

Sometime, somehow the current universe
emerged. Gravity pulled hydrogen into gas clouds.
Protons and electrons dispersed the fog.
"Reionization" was the last major transition.
This is one of the frontiers of astrophysics.

Without light it is hard to probe the Dark Ages.
But they study the first quasars surrounding
supermassive black holes. This new discovery
opens more speculation on how black holes
grow more quickly. Are older black holes
waiting to be found?

Baflados said, "At some point these should
not exist. When is that point? We still don't know."
We may not exist long enough to ever know.
In another dimension we might get to know.
Was there ever a time that nothing existed?
Well, in this life cycle at least it is a mental fog
not the chilly, featureless fog of eons ago.

Gleaning Global Gaps

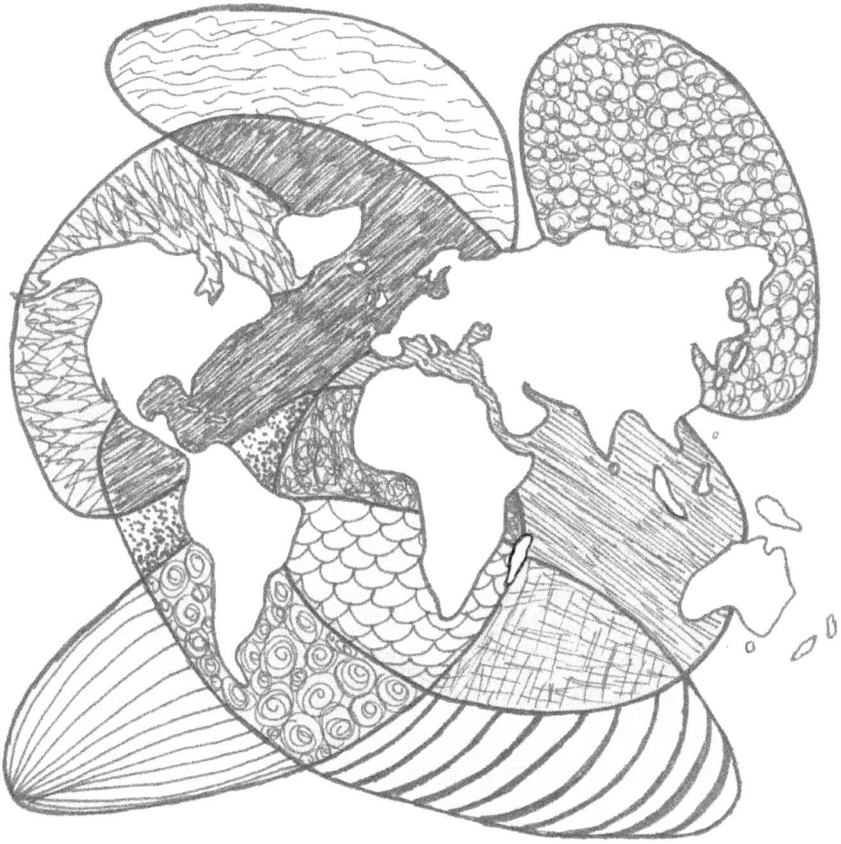

If you find a need, fulfill the gap.

Lailah Gifty Akita

I Wonder Why

Listening to the news I wonder why
this September is especially hard?
Why is the world in such short supply–
with safety, compassion thin? We bombard
toward each other with lethal blasts
such suffering that lasts and lasts.

This September is especially hard
as hurricanes, wildfires, earthquakes, human error,
flood, burn, shake, destroy, disregard--
bringing evacuations, devastation, horror.
Events drown or choke
traumatic to effected folk.

Why is the world in such short supply
of safeguards, bandages, restraints
forcing fighters and helpers to occupy,
rescue, handle dire complaints?
The damage is incalculable.
Losses to all beings unimaginable.

With safety, compassion thin, we bombard
governmental and charitable agencies
to alleviate what is irretrievable in our backyard,
appealing to basic decencies.
There's just so much we can heed
when there is such desperate need.

Toward each other with lethal blasts
we add war, threats of aerial EMP*.
Nature is not enough. All flabbergasts
at the insanity of aspects of humanity.
Surrounded by hazards beyond our control,
how do we contribute? Play positive role?

Such suffering that lasts and lasts
wearies hope, brings serotinal gloom.
People choke compromised air's overcast-
a heavy pall as angst mushrooms.
Facing conditions of such severity
the world yearns for return of relief, levity.

* Electro-magnetic pulse which could fry power grid.

176

Disconnected?

A hurricane of theories twist and twirl
about our rapidly spiraling future.
Puzzle pieces don't connect- swirl.
No stability in any earthly culture.
Are we part of some galactic war?
Will we gain our freedom once more?

About our rapidly spiraling future,
the forecasts see old ways crumbling.
Upheavals in nature, rifts without suture,
few solutions to our bumbling.
Like Shiva- destroy and renew?
What's life like when we are through?

Puzzle pieces don't connect- swirl
around trying to fit into place.
We're caught in a tilt-a-whirl.
What's the destiny for the human race?
Whose in charge of our codes?
Are our technologies making inroads?

No stability in any earthly culture
governed by oppressive leadership goals
divisive positions, rising temperature,
too many people, too few good roles.
Have we awakened enough to new vibration?
Stay in revolution or stagnation?

Are we part of some galactic war?
Good and evil forces wanting our domain?
Will we rejoin some group more stellar?
Will we reform and reclaim this plane?
Are we shifting to a high frequency
with more sustaining decency?

Will we gain our freedom once more
from outside intervention so we can evolve?
What is the planet's enduring metaphor?
Vibrate our power to enlighten and solve
Gaia's viability and humanity's distress?
Will we remain mired in this mess?

Shifting Through Dimensions

After the solar eclipse many mention
they anticipate a dimensional shift.
They hope to rise to the fifth dimension
to give humanity and Gaia a lift.
>Our guides and angels might exchange
>to harmonize to our new vibe range.

They anticipate a dimensional shift
to a higher frequency and to be lighter.
This process could create a rift
between 3D folk and 5D when brighter.
>But our support staff entered at our birth
>may face a changing of the guard, new berth.

They hope to rise to the fifth dimension.
Perhaps it will save Earth and inhabitants?
Eagerly they await ascension,
the elimination of 3D irritants.
>The planet can then replenish and restore
>to a sustainable, beautiful place once more.

To give humanity and Gaia a lift
people must raise their vibration.
Will otherworldly beings help uplift
to help us with our liberation?
>Is this idea just a pipe dream?
>Or is it less outlandish than it may seem?

Our guides and angels might exchange
posts to another 3D posting.
If 5D contingent takes over with change,
an enlightened species they may be hosting.
>Our cosmic crew needs to vibrate with us.
>The transfer would be miraculous.

To harmonize to our new vibe range,
requires an upgrade of frequency, mind and heart.
When the Old World Order appears strange–
a New World?   I want to be a part.
>Whoever is with me in another realm,
>I welcome whoever takes the helm.

The Week that Was...

From the Great American Solar Eclipse
to the week of the Fall Equinox
we have dire predictions from several sources.

Today September 23rd is the apocalypse
according to some dark folks. I hope not.
It is our grandson's 22nd birthday.

On the equinox, supposedly,
5D energy whacked humanity
which really made some feel walloped.

The week around the equinox was
intense solar flares, wildfires, hurricanes,
massive earthquakes and political chaos.

Trump thumps the United Nations.
"Rocket Man" and "Dotard" exchange
insults and escalate threats of war.

Congress debates health care again, depriving
millions access. I called to thank McCain and Rand,
and urged the two on-edge women to vote no.

Our Huddle gathered on the equinox to discuss
the Russian hacking, environmental and political
problems we needed to address.

It was also International Peace Day. I wore
my safety pin to declare everyone is safe with me–
even though I do not feel safe...even in Corvallis.

Nationally, people are in the streets protesting injustice,
inequality. Confederate monuments face removal,
Education Department and EPA propose regressive measures.

This afternoon when gray clouds supposedly lift
and the damp chill lessens, we hope to go to Fall Festival
with arts and crafts–an uplifting focus.

My husband planted grass seed on the cherry tree's grave.
Sprinkler sprays until recent rains resume in a few days.
This afternoon I'll welcome sun, warmth, delight, joy...hopefully.

Ecological Roulette

Scientists...tracked the species to their Japanese origins. Their arrival could be a problem if the critters take root, pushing out native species. It's a bit of what we call ecological roulette.   James Carlton

Nearly 300 species of fish, mussels,
other sea creatures hitchhiked
across the Pacific Ocean on debris, tussles
with local species. Newcomers disliked.
    From 2011 Japanese tsunami to our shore,
    invasive species come to explore.

Other sea creatures hitchhiked.
A million creatures traveled 4,800 miles.
Hundreds of thousands of mussels not liked,
join global invasive species problem, while
    hurt native farmed shellfish, erode
    local ecosystems, economic losses explode.

Across the Pacific Ocean on debris, tussles
with mollusks, sea anemones, crabs, coral
which carry diseases on currents, arrives and out-muscles
the native species thriving in that locale.
    Now species travel in a plastic flotilla, not wood.
    Buoys, boats, crates, pallets of plastic could.

With local species, newcomers disliked.
Plastic debris allows species to survive longer.
A natural trigger and plastic hiked
amazing survival, diversity stronger.
    Who will win the desired slot?
    Which species will not?

From 2011 Japanese tsunami to our shore--
Oregon and Washington most heavily hit,
invaders become a tragic metaphor.
Alaska and California also hit.
    A small boat had 20 good-sized fish.
    See them in an aquarium if you wish.

Invasive species come to explore
place to where they were displaced.
Parasites are found in gills of mussels, more
problems for scientists and species faced.
    We spin turbulence on a plastic wheel.
    Will we have time to heal?

Plastics Shall Inherit the Earth

Industry has made 9.1 billion tons of plastic since 1960 and there's enough left over to bury Manhattan under more than two miles of trash. Plastics don't break down like other man-made materials, so three-quarters of the stuff ends up as waste in landfills, littered on land, and floating in oceans, lakes and rivers. At the current rate we are really heading toward a plastic planet. Seth Borenstein

Before plastics, things recycled into the earth
or disintegrated in time in the sea,
people didn't shoot as much pollution to the air.

After plastics made the scene, it
was too durable, disposable–tossed
everywhere. Now it could overtake us.

Since people make plastics and the data
is so depressing, the enduring plastics
could remain long after we had to depart.

Garbage used to compost. Now plastic chunks,
garbage gyres in the sea, litter everywhere.
I need to check if my home will gobble me up.

My husband recycles every possible item.
He re-purposes and is careful what he purchases.
He is an excellent steward of Gaia-- plastic protester.

I did a survey of the plastics I contributed
to our home environment. Most of my debris
is storage containers for paper products.

Oops, a plastic ruler. Plastic pens. Plastic glasses
the ones on my face. I prefer glass for drinking.
What about some beverage containers? Packaging?

I no longer buy plasticware, plates or cups
for parties, weaning to metal drinking containers.
We'll see what 3D printing will bring. Maybe recyclable?

Even some of the angels in my collection
are plastic–but they're my least favorite than fabric,
wood or ceramic. Plastic angels are mostly gifts.

My other collectibles are wood folk art
and mostly felt Annalees. Fairies and elves,
old dolls are PC and not PC as plastic correct.

But, oh gosh, polyester clothes and my beautiful
blue Fit–plastic gobblers. I am engulfed in plastic!
Even pill bottles, phones, remotes, spiral bindings...etc.

Only 9 percent of plastic got recycled, 12 percent
incinerated, 7 billion tons no longer used.
5.5 billion tons of plastic waste on land and in water.

Plastic promoters say using alternatives for packaging
and consumer goods requires more energy. Plastics
are efficient, cost effective and do their jobs.

The world makes more steel and concrete,
but they stay longer and degrade better.
Plastics stick around and become waste quickly.

Plastic is just one of the products messing
up the Anthropocene era. Not the poor will
inherit the Earth–but nature plagued by plastic.

Trashing Henderson Island

It speaks to the fact that these items that we call "disposable" or "single-use" are neither of those things and that items constructed decades ago are still floating in the ocean for days and for decades to come. Dr. Jennifer Lavers

Henderson Island in the South Pacific
is a UNESCO World Heritage Site
chosen in 1998 because it was largely
untouched by humans and had rare ecology.

38 million pieces of trash washed
upon its pristine shores. White sands
speckled with multi-colored, mostly plastic
trash mostly from China, Japan and Chile.

Henderson Island is one of the last two
raised coral atolls covered with 17.6 tons
of debris. The world produces that much
plastic every 1.98 seconds. Where will it land?

53,000 pieces mostly of plastic from bottles,
cigarette lighters, fishing gear–most buried
in the sand, but much splayed over the beach, near
the western side of South Pacific Gyre debris dump

Rare ecology threatened. Ten of 51 flowering plants,
all four land birds, 1/3 of insects and gastropods
are endemic–a remarkable diversity for such
a small island, dumped on by absentee humans.

Perhaps humans should start a clean-up,
recycle as they are trying to do with ocean-trapped
debris all over the planet. Can we sieve the trash
someday before it washes ashore or inflicts oceans.

Perhaps we can recycle before it hits water,
pollutes our seas and threatens sea life?
Can we restore Henderson Island to be
the World Heritage site it was intended to showcase?

Fatbergs

Sewer spies use remote cameras to find
congealed lumps of fat clogging sewer pipes.
Fatbergs in pipes weigh tons and remind
population pressures toss different types
       of gunk into outdated sewer systems.
       We create fatbergs with bogging items.

Congealed lumps of fat clogging sewer pipes
contain fats, oils, grease which harden and collect
even diapers and flushable wet wipes.
Some things don't break down, remain a smelly object.
       London's fatberg weighs 11 double-decker buses.
       A Baltimore fatberg blocks 85% of pipe-incredulous.

Fatbergs in pipes weigh tons and remind
both cities' sewer infrastructures are very old.
Baltimore faces another sewer problem–the kind
where 1.2 million gallons of sewage overflowed.
       Both cities are chipping away at the enormous fat
       with shovels and high pressure hoses to combat.

Population pressures toss different types
of debris which will have to be shipped to landfills or a museum.
A museum could display horrid smell and gripes
with fatberg chunks in sealed containers so visitors can see them.
       Another way fat is up close and personal.
       Sewers serve a messy clientele.

Of gunk into outdated sewer systems,
we have just explored tips of icebergs.
We are discovering disturbing omens,
with these disgusting fatbergs.
       Where will all this waste go?
       How can we keep the flow?

We create fatbergs with bogging items.
Restaurants and residents are urged to avoid
putting fats, oils, grease, wet wipes in sewer to stem
clogs. If not, everyone could be very annoyed.
       Only flushable toilet paper, poo and pee
       will keep systems moving smoothly.

Tunneling

A shallower than Onkalo nuclear site incident
occurred at Hanford Nuclear Reservation.
Onkalo is deep within the earth in Finland,
but they fear one day a leak might surface.

In a 360-foot-long tunnel built in 1956
eight flatbed railroad cars loaded with about
780 cubic yards of waste– radioactive
and chemical waste, irradiated equipment.

A sinkhole caved in the tunnel.
8-feet of dirt protected eight irradiated
carriers of spent nuclear fuel rods.
Sinkhole's hole open for probably four days.

20-foot by 20-foot hole in the roof
of a storage tunnel caused evacuations
and evaluation of inspection procedures.
No one hurt. No radiation escaped.

All these nuclear moles tunneling
the earth, risking leaks into the air
and contamination of the Columbia River.
Any light at the end of the tunnel?

Invading the Doomsday Vault

The Svalbard Global Seed Bank
preserving over 1 million varieties of seed packets
in the event of a natural or global disaster
was breached by permafrost melt.

Buried deep in a mountain in Svalbard
archipelago in Norway, 1,300 kilometers
from the North Pole, the vault was considered
failsafe in impenetrable deep frost: food supply forever.

But 2016 had the highest arctic temperatures on record
and the permafrost melted into the entrance tunnel,
turning to ice like a glacier before reaching the seeds.
The seeds safe for now at -18C storage temperature.

New protections are needed if humanity is to use
the seeds after catastrophe–if either seeds
or people survive. The ice was hacked out.
The vault monitored 24/7. Seeds preserved.

They hope someday the seed bank can
take care of itself. But maybe no one survives
to seed or protect the seed. Maybe it will
get so hot, water will gush in and drown all.

International Day of Peace

We cannot live in a world where wearing a sign of our faith–a hijab or a
yarmulke, a cross or a collar carries with it the threat of harm.
Matt Caro, Bob Hornstein, Emmett Wheatfall

Not just faith symbols bring violence and fear.
It's the swastika, white hoods, Confederate flags,
so many organizations identified as threats–
labeling people as "other" with diverse beliefs–
not always religious, perhaps ideological.
We are divided, disconnected globally.

The Peace Day theme for the United Nations
is "Together" which promotes respect, safety
and dignity for everyone who has been forced
to flee their homes for a better life....but
we have climate change refugees, travel bans,
DACA debate, Myanmar mass exodus, African
and Middle Eastern emigrants from poverty and war.

North Korea poses danger of nuclear war.
Leadership in many governments ineffective,
incompetent, power hungry at expense of country.
TV programs upset us with bloody portrayals.
The lies, deceit, distrust is global.
The inequities, arousals of hate are horrifying.

Ken Burn's documentary on Viet Nam reveals
cover-ups and covert actions with misleading
motives on all sides– the senseless slaughter,
misguided bravery, unnecessary pain, wrenching.
Sometimes I just do not want to know the past
atrocities and present happenings. It overwhelms.

They say people of peace should stand up to hate.
Mentally deranged people, traumatized people
do not sit down if you stand. Violence breeds violence.
Protests face anti-protests. People die from difference
and indifference. Respecting some despicable people,
forgive and forget mode–I have not reached that level.

Some believe every human being is created in the image
of God or a Creator. Why would a Creator create
such a cruel experiment? Is peace even innate?
Do we learn kindness only by witnessing suffering?
I find earthly expectations in duality and 3D–disappointing.
I stand on my cranky knees in peaceful protest to this warped world.

Flaming Hell

If humanity is to continue another million years, humans must "boldly go where no one has gone beforebefore." To leave Earth demands a concerted global approach. Everyone should join in. Stephen Hawking

Hawking predicts we have 600 years before
becoming a sizzling fireball due to over-crowding,
and energy consumption. The planet
will be uninhabitable by 2600 from population
pressures and energy demands.

Humanity faces threats from climate change,
nuclear war destruction, genetically engineered
viruses, over-population straining resources.
We need to get off the planet before
it consumes us in a ball of fire.

Elon Musk concurs we face a mass extinction
event which will wipe out humanity on Earth.
Hawking is working with Mark Zuckerberg
in Breakthrough Starshot to send a probe
to the nearest star system Alpha Centauri.

They will use an ultra-fast, light-powered
spacecraft to look for habitable worlds
in Alpha Centauri. It takes less than an hour
to Mars–but twenty years to Alpha Centauri.
If lucky, can we get there in time?

Hawking estimates we have 100 years
and our future is not on the planet we treated
poorly, polluted unsustainably. Would we
do the same elsewhere? Would they allow
us to stay? Would we all go? Lottery?

If we escape Flaming Hell, would we have
learned how to become a cosmic citizen
adding positivity to the life forces in the cosmos?
Is there a place for us to start again? In what form?
A.I. advanced? Still fragile,fleshy? New breed human?

Perhaps our species blew our Earth-bound
experiment and do not merit another chance?
Perhaps more intelligent species will inhabit
worlds suitable to them? We are left out?
Escaping Flaming Hell for Ideal Heaven–delusion?

Searching for Yonies

Yonies mean positive vibes.

A summary of the 15,000 Second Notice scientists' report
suggests our doom from climate change and mass extinction
because there are too many of us consuming out of control.

By failing to adequately limit population growth, reassess
the role of an economy rooted in growth, reduce greenhouse
gases, incenticize renewable energy, protect habitat, restore
ecosystems, curb pollution, halt defaunation, constrain
evasive societies, humanity is not taking the urgent steps
to safeguard our imperiled biosphere.

The few yonies: ozone layer better and preventing
millions of cases of skin cancer, reduction in extreme
poverty and hunger. Still seems a long way to go.

As individuals we can: have fewer children (replacement
of two tops), don't waste and eat mostly plant-based food,
(less cow and sheep), buy green, appreciate and support nature.

Government and nations can do their part.
With current US administration as role models,
we will not lead the world toward sustainability.

We need environmentally aware economies,
to stop wiping out ecosystems and animal species,
to develop green technologies and more nature preserves.

How about more yonies for love, compassion,
justice, peace, equity, kindness, ban violence
and weapons, promote cooperation not competition.

Each of us can be aware of the yonies we exude,
work toward the positive and confront the negative.
Yonies is a made-up word. What will we be made of?

Smog

Smog rolls around the world–
every continent, killing millions.
India, Iran, China are not alone
suffering from pollution.

As we despoil air, land and water,
how are we to breathe, drink,
grow food to sustain us?

Has humanity lost its will to live?
Are we too weak-willed to confront
climate change, waste, degradation?

With Obama I had hope humanity
might wake up and change, but Trump
stomps our best intentions.

Perhaps the 99% will attack the 1%
in a revolution for equity and justice.
Greed and irresponsibility are killing us.

Small victories must become larger.
Gaia is gasping. Either Gaia or the cosmos
could cease our existence, take breath away.

Humanity needs to earn privilege to stay,
must sustain not destroy. So many of us
are world-weary. Life too heavy to lift?

Smog smothers. A warning.
How many creatures must die,
before we all do?

Warning to Humanity

Human beings and the natural world are on a collision course. Human activities inflict harsh and often irreversible damage on the environment and on critical resources. If not checked, many of our current practices put at serious risk the future that we wish for human society and the plant and animal kingdoms, and may so alter the living world that it will be unable to sustain life in the manner that we know. Fundamental changes are urgent if we are to avoid the collision our present course will bring about.

1,700 world scientists in November 1992

Since then the widening hole in the ozone layer
has been largely fixed, but otherwise we are worse off
due to our pollution, destruction of air, land and sea.

Climate change warming is denied by some, but
the effects on weather and planet are undeniable.
Humanity is the accelerator. Time for some brakes.

Too many people for too few resources, disregard
for waste disposal and destruction of habitats.
Seas clogged. Air and land also contaminated.

When will we not breathe, eat or drink? Get crispy?
Some groups work hard to protect and heal
Earth's global problems, but in time before extinction?

Sometimes I think humanity has had its run
on Gaia and we were not the stewards we should be.
The planet will survive, but not all life on it.

In time when Gaia has recovered, new starseeds
could arrive, adapt to conditions, with the goal
of sustaining life with higher intentions and cooperation.

Humanity's soul-slivers could go into cosmic rehab.
Depending on their progress they could go
to another multiversal location. Will we be forgiven?

2018 is an 11 Year

Don't be fooled by the further chaos, trickery and general darkness of politics and big business. The world will continue to spin and turn. However, this year YOU have the option to opt out of the drama. It doesn't mean not to stand up for light. Sara Wiseman

Apparently as 2018 is an 11 year, this is a year to focus
on intuition, spirituality and your inner you or soul.
We are embroiled in a sleight of the hand hocus-pocus,
stuck in bureaucracy and disingenuous rigamarole.
> It is hard to look within when around you, you witness
> violence, oppression, division, injustice.

On intuition, spirituality and your inner you or soul,
apparently remember what affects one affects the One,
so while digging inward, you have a light-bringing role.
Are we to go passively into extinction?
> We are told not to feel we are not enough
> and we are already whole– seek blissful stuff.

We are embroiled in a sleight of the hand hocus-pocus,
leadership by greed not constituents' needs.
We are integrally connected–all of us.
We watch in horror as the world burns and bleeds.
> When news arrives shedding some light,
> we feel a respite in our global plight.

Stuck in bureaucracy and disingenuous rigamarole,
are the advances to help relieve suffering.
Whatever the issue and results of votes or poll,
little gets done, but huff and puffering.
> Certain leaders are insane,
> leaving people to feel the pain.

It is hard to look within when around you you witness
so much to challenge- no time to stare at your navel.
Since we are whole and enough, we have the fitness
to help Gaia, enlighten or will we unravel?
> Can we step back, drop out, withdraw?
> I'm distracted, overwhelmed, too cold to thaw.

Violence, oppression, division, injustice
are omnipresent as I seek to breathe bliss.
Would a little hope and kindness suffice?
Did I reincarnate to learn from this?
> Apparently only inner change matters–forever?
> Does a soul never get to say "never"?

Protesting Unfulfilled Gaps

Never be afraid to raise your voice
for honesty and truth and compassion
against injustice, lying and greed.
If people all over the world
would do this, it would change the world.

William Faulkner

Raise Your Words and Voice

Raise your words, not voice. It is rain that grows flowers, not thunder.
Jalaluddin Rumi

In protest marches we raise signs.
We chant in a loud voice.
We advocate for our designs.
We want peace, freedom of choice.
       Progressive changes if we are to exist.
       We will persist and resist.

We chant in a loud voice:
active participants for climate change.
We don't want destruction's invoice.
Priorities we'd like to rearrange:
       equity, justice, help for disability.
       If racist, sexist, ageist–take responsibility.

We advocate for our designs
for a sustainable, better future.
Differences? Way that intertwines?
Rid ourselves of xenophobic culture.
       We discuss ideas in our Huddle
       to get us out of this muddle.

We want peace, freedom of choice,
a more gentle civilization.
More time to create and rejoice,
come to a hopeful realization.
       Pollution, extinctions run rampant.
       Will our world still be extant?

Progressive changes if we are to exist
start at grassroots, demand leadership actions.
Perhaps we need an exorcist
to achieve our satisfactions?
       We need a attitude correction
       to make a better connection.

We will persist and resist.
Leaders are taking us down the wrong path.
We must unite and insist
we don't have a devastating aftermath.
       Citizens are waking up in throngs,
       challenging everyone to right the wrongs.

Language of Resistance

The resistance really resonates with me...Let's look at what language is doing, what it enables us to get away with, but also how it invites us to what might be needed... Poetry as a bridge for people of different backgrounds and viewpoints. Tracy K. Smith

Protests explode in signs and social media,
President's ignorant tweets enrage us.
Politicians propose outrageous ideas.
Satire and comedy engage us.
      TV and newspapers display images which make
      for us to question whether they are real or fake.

President's ignorant tweets enrage us.
The babyish, whiney bully can't spell.
His whole administration continues to muss
up all the programs Obama did well.
      Trump faces several serious charges.
      We hope justice rightfully discharges.

Politicians propose outrageous ideas,
defund health care, environment, education.
Globally we are off-base in many areas.
We're in untrusted, laughing stock situation.
      The majority did not vote for him.
      The hope for a turn-around is slim.

Satire and comedy engage us,
We laugh at ourselves through tears.
Protesters march and cause a ruckus.
The whole world seems in arrears.
      To sustain a world of stability
      requires leadership with ability.

TV and newspapers display images which make
us wonder what to support and believe.
So much blood and heartbreak
with no solutions to relieve.
      Some nations show signs of progress.
      We must persist for further success.

For us to question whether they are real or fake
demands open flow, not hacked information.
We can't allow evil actions to overtake
our attempts for sustainable reformation.
      Our words, heard, seen or spoken
      can uplift and keep spirits unbroken.

Sign For The TImes

Wherever you're from, we're glad you are our neighbor. Lawn sign

On Mother's Day our son gave us a lawn sign,
with a "safety pin" message to stake in our yard.
Three languages are part of the design.
Deciphering words in two languages for me is hard.
> The message is of unity, oneness and peace.
> A global vibration we could release.

With safety pin message to stake in our yard
like "safe with me" symbol pinned to our chests,
espouses positive "isms" to hold in regard--
words of hope, kindness, tolerance sign suggests.
> Striped in green, blue and orange like a flag,
> with bright lettering for when spirits lag.

Three languages are part of the design
calligraphic alphabets flow like art.
A patch in a global quilt–this one mine.
I'm proud to show it, take part.
> Think of all places flaring messages of love.
> Think of all the positive acts we're capable of.

Deciphering words in two languages for me is hard.
One is Spanish and one Arabic not Chinese.
I assume they all say the same on this placard.
I can only read the English layer with ease.
> Walkers can read it as they pass by.
> Gawkers from cars could give it a try.

The message of unity, oneness and peace
highlights connection, cooperation.
An urgent message speaks its piece.
We're all in this together–every nation.
> If we gather together, regardless of culture,
> we could create a joyous future.

A global vibration we could release,
energizing actions for sustainability,
and responsibility. Can we hurry up, please
so each of us can contribute to one's best ability?
> The sign of the times could be a peace symbol,
> ushering in a non-violent, world-wide protocol.

Slacktivism

Actions taken to bring about political or social change, but requiring only
minimal commitment, effort or risk.   Dictionary.com

Writing the Wrongs to Rights Huddle
composed mostly of children's book writers
and poets formed in response
to the Women's March movement
and to Persist and Resist Trump.

We have monthly meetings,
but forward e-mails for petitions
and political events to the group.
We have participated in marches,
attended town halls, met with Congressmen,
sent Ides of Trump postcards, written editorials,
e-mails to DC politicians,
attend local meetings of town government
and lobby state level as well.
Some are on committees and are part
of organizations working for change.
Some send money to their causes.
The Huddles contribute any way they can.
We formed sub-committees on various issues
to research and share information.
We try to keep the lines of communication open,
read and listen to news sources.
We are getting information from so many
protest groups, we feel overwhelmed.

Some of the efforts might be considered
slacktivism. Members have various reasons
why their activism is hampered, but
all earnestly want to support peace, justice,
the environment, health care for all, women,
respect for all people... the list goes on and on.

The hearts and minds are activist.
The bodies might be slacktivist.
Our mission is urgent. As David Brook says:
"We've got this perverse situation in which
the vast analytic powers of the entire world
are being spent trying to understand a guy
whose thoughts are often just six fireflies
beeping randomly in a jar".
The whole world needs activists
to energize the slacktivists.

The Good Samaritans

Rick John Best, Taliesin Myrddin Namkai-Meche, Micah David-Cole Fletcher

Two teenage girls riding on the MAX train--
one black and one wearing a hijab--
they were terrorized by an extremist, who again
publicly espoused his views, began to stab
        three men who came to the girls' defense.
        Jeremy Christian committed the offense.

One black and one wearing a hijab,
the girls cringed from the racist vitriol.
The assailant, three men tried to grab
killed two men and injured the other, overall
        shocked everyone. Heroes tested.
        Extremist chased and was arrested.

They were terrorized by an extremist, who again
attacked with Nazi beliefs, anti-Muslim memes.
This time violently, lethally inflicted pain,
but not so unexpected as it seems.
        On Facebook and rallies he expressed his views.
        Could we have acted differently with these clues?

Publicly espoused his views, began to stab,
lashing out like he did at March for Free Speech.
He has a long rap sheet. How many times must we nab
such a dangerous criminal, now with this breach
        taking two lives causing terror in Portland?
        Why this has to happen, I don't understand.

Three men who came to the girls' defense
--a veteran, recent Reed graduate, only poet survived--
honored by community, Muslim leaders recompense.
Police didn't shoot killer. When confronted, he lived.
        Passengers screaming, streaming from cars,
        leaving a community with fear and scars.

Jeremy Christian committed the offense
in a national climate of increased hate.
Terrorism inflamed at opponents' expense.
Such behavior we can't tolerate.
        Most Oregonians grieve this Ramadan day.
        Most Oregonians believe in a loving way.

Standing Up for Each Other

*There are so many times, and so many ways, to stand up for the right of people
who are different to exist on this planet, and to exist on this particular piece of
this planet.* David Sarasohn

Chalk messages, photographs, poems, handwritten notes
graffiti the walls in Portland, Oregon beside candles
a military cap, candles, stuffed animals and flowers.

"Love Portland (the Real Portland)"
"Out of a great need we are all holding hands."
"Portland...We have to do better."

Portland responds to a man slashing three men
who rose to protect two teen girls from racial abuse.
One man, a poet, survived by a combat veteran's skill.

Michah Fletcher the knife slash surviver says,
"We must protect each other, like that is the truth
no matter what the consequences."

The Washington Post headlines: Portland often
seen as a progressive playground, now confronts
murderous hate, claims Portland has racism in its blood.

I do not believe Portlandia is basically racist
as it was in the past. Weird Portland is a green,
dreamer's place with challenges we face everywhere.

Portland is in pain, stunned by the evil
unnerving the city and spreading globally.
Remember more people march for good causes.

Marcus Knipe, whose fingers held Fletcher's wound
said "We must all stand up for each other".
"Help me find the courage" one note asked the universe.

Freedom of speech promoting hate
and assault on others' difference
is not acceptable in a democratic society.

Why must we rally in grief, leave pieces of ourselves
at memorials when we know they are transitory
and soon we will be grieving again?

Our messages blow in the wind, flowers fade,
chalk smudges, washes off. Candles burn out.
Portland is not alone facing terrorism and hate.

Ron Wyden Town Hall
   May 27, 2017 Philomath High School Gym

Senator Wyden spoke in Salem before coming to Philomath
for his 821st town hall since he took office.
It is the Saturday of Memorial Day weekend.
A warm, sunny day- a holiday, yet hundreds came,
filled the gym, greeted him with a standing ovation.
This was not a Republican Town Hall. This is Oregon.

We signed in and received a ticket if we wanted to speak.
I wrote my organization as Writing the Wrongs Huddle.
The Senator started with the stabbings in Portland.
A man confronted and verbally abused two women
he believed Muslim, then stabbed to death two defenders.
Wyden had spoken to one of the grieving mothers,
asked the audience to observe a moment of silence.

Then from 2:30 - 4, he answered questions from the public,
talked about what he supported and how he would do so.
Questions on health care: Mark Weiss sang about the need
for a single payer system. Wyden had not been sung
to before at a town hall and suggested Rachel Maddow
hear it. He opposes cuts to medicare and for the wealthy.

Questions about vote by mail, DeVos disaster education,
selling Internet privacy, encouraging younger participation,
science lab cuts, Russian influence and ways to indict Trump
and his cronies, 2020 census and be sure it is done fairly, etc.
So many thanked him for coming and his progressive votes.
His work on environment, intelligence, health care and tax reform.

He took an extra question after they told him time was up.
A young Muslim man had walked from Corvallis to Philomath,
on Ramadan in the high 80's heat to tell him of the hate
and terrorism many Muslims and minorities were facing.
Wyden is a Jew and he is a Muslim. He pleaded
to see all sides work together for tolerance and freedom.

Wyden began and ended by his heart-felt defense
of advocating from a grassroots level to turn this country around.
The supportive audience stood again, applauding his efforts.
Tomorrow he goes to Florence #822. We walked into sun.
Many in the crowd knew each other and felt proud we had
a senator who listens and acts for the good of constituents.

Dealing With the News

Morning newspapers blur my vision.
Evening TV news stabs my heart.
What is true news? Fake news position?
Whatever source, news tears me apart.
        Should I stop watching the news?
        What would happen if I refuse?

Evening TV news stabs my heart–
some comic relief, satire late night,
still global pain hits me like a dart
as I witness environment's and people's plight.
        I feel I need to know what's going on,
        but I feel manipulated, preyed upon.

What is true news? Fake news position?
So much to sift and check resources.
This is a considerable time imposition.
How do we find the best resources?
        Good news? Bad news? Depends on views.
        Certain issues get divided reviews.

Whatever source, news tears me apart.
I miss progressive, competent Obama calm.
Now regressive, incompetent, chaotic counterpart.
I can't envision a near future balm.
        Too much greed, deceit, hacking.
        Too many politicians whose integrity's lacking.

Should I stop watching the news?
De-stress with handling information
that uplifts, poses solutions, clues
for better ways to reach a destination?
        How do we find positive consensus
        with so many negative expenses?

What would happen if I refuse
to protect myself—more importantly–
how can my actions be of effective use?
I can't proceed ignorantly.
        My jangled nerves and popped eyes
        will have to wait for the next surprise.

A Tiki Torch in Charlottesville

I'm burned. What am I doing in a Unite the Right protest
at the University of Virginia? Supposed to oppose
the takedown of some Confederate statue?

I'm burned like KKK torches. But I am
a backyard party decor– to brighten the dark,
I'm supposed to lighten things up.

I'm burned these violent men carry me with shields,
sticks and guns–weapons they think they need
to protect themselves, yet they attack.

I'm burned one Nazi rams and injures anti-haters
with a car and kills a young woman–
a cowardly, evil, dastardly deed.

I'm burned by a man with a heavy, sweaty hand.
Torches sweep like a forest fire through campus,
emblazoned by racist and religious hatred.

I'm burned, but expose the uncovered faces
of these hate groups with angry
countenances shouting hateful slogans.

I'm burned as they march. Still igniting crosses?
Lynching? They march without white coverups,
emboldened by Trump and the alt-right.

I'm burned but enhance light for cell phones to snap
pictures of haters and post torch-lit faces
on the Internet for viewers to identify and name.

I'm burned like Statue of Liberty torch. A tiki torch
carrier taking liberty from others is exposed.
Tiki-light cost many men their jobs—fired.

I'm burned this man picked me up
for this sordid affair. What darkness
did he bring to light? Why such hate?

I'm burned, inflamed about what made
this white man turn dark, wanting to burn
and harm others. I'm not one of his weapons.

I'm burned. Maybe I'll be declared an unwelcome import,
but I'm made in USA. I do not want any more of us
to become a hate symbol in another night terror event.

I'm burned. I hope I'm not coming to your town unless
I can be a light of your party, pest deterrent, igniter
of barbecue... I'm burned out with haters.

Fading Moral Values

Moral: 1.relating to the principles of right and wrong. 2.conforming to a standard of right behavior. capable of right and wrong action. 3. probable, but not proven. 4. perceptual or psychological rather than tangible or practical in nature or effect.

The Gallop Poll found 80% of people polled
rated U.S. values at fair to poor and getting worse.
Guess it's how you define morals. Poll told
no matter one's outlook, others seen perverse.
> Political and cultural camps agree.
> They view our country's morals dimly.

Rated U.S. values at fair to poor and getting worse?
Just how did Gallup select their sample
to find so many people's propensity adverse?
Polls were wrong on 2016 election for example.
> The divides crack open, deepen perspective.
> We take sides and find some people defective.

Guess it's how you define morals. Poll told
moderates, liberals, conservatives all dissatisfied.
All are unhappy with turn of events and scold.
How will these downfalls be rectified?
> Ethics and moral standards vary
> which leaves many people wary.

No matter one's outlook, others seen perverse.
If they do not think like you, they must be wrong?
Our wayward ways concern of universe?
Our ingrained convictions remain strong.
> Can we all agree anything is good or evil?
> All thought and action pounded on anvil?

Political and cultural camps agree
we are facing difficult times, destruction
of values, environment, democracy.
Justice fights corruption and obstruction.
> Listen to the news and you wish it were fake.
> How much negativity can the populace take?

They view our country's morals dimly.
Inequality, inequities, lack of responsibility persist.
No wonder we perceive our morality grimly.
The question is now, how do we resist?
> Are morals restrictive of individual choice?
> Do morals give well-intentioned folks a voice?

A New Story

Futurist thinkers suggest separation
is the source of alienation
across the globe and in our nation.

We need a new story
not based on old glory,
more gentle, less gory.

People are feeling confused
through media they are infused
with conflicting data and feel used.

People want a sense of connection
not competition, but cooperation,
a sense of justice and protection.

The old ways are crumbling
due to our bumbling,
leaving us grumbling.

Politicians don't appear wise,
don't want to compromise,
Greed, power they prize.

Things happen out of our control.
Regulations lessened, no one to patrol.
Lots of malpractice out on parole.

We want to connect to a good cause,
toward more toward equity, justice because
good intentions deserve applause.

We see unraveling of The American Dream
despite best efforts it comes apart at the seams.
The reality is, it's not what it seems.

Time to sustain, not spoil,
regulate coal and oil
not poison and frack soil.

We can't pollute land, sea and air
so life can't thrive anywhere.
In time, can people care and share?

Health care is a human right.
Time for Congress to unite
make one-payer plan, end divisive fight.

If separation is cause of hatred and fear,
can kind, giving connections appear
to create a more positive atmosphere?

We must join the Paris Accord
improve our destructive record,
mediation and diplomacy heard.

Why can't we work together to explore space
to avoid waste of a space race,
together we'd increase the pace.

But we can't abandon needs of folks below,
we're stewards of the Earth, you know
and must try to avoid a final blow.

As we move to 4th Industrial Revolution,
we face disruption and disillusion,
we should work for a sustainable conclusion.

Some say we face a 6th extinction,
creating the first distinction
of people ending planet's habitation.

Some say we are upgrading to fifth dimension,
perhaps hopeful for some suspension
of our errant ways into redemption.

Can we innovate a new framework,
plug connections in a useful network?
Just who will do the work?

Separation is a lonely force,
causing maladies, divorce--
needs remedies, of course.

But the new story involves billions
as we diminish wildlife by millions,
and the costs balloon into trillions.

The challenges break my heart.
Who wants to stand apart?
Who will take the courage to start?

Cyber Attacks

A global cyber attack infected
computers around the world with malware.
The kill switch accidentally detected.
Hero frees from WannaCry ransomware.
> In 100 countries cyber-attacking,
> cause of dangerous hacking.

Computers around the world with malware
from a loophole in Microsoft systems,
made globally-linked users aware
of leaking of their digital items.
> Hackers demand ransom to get bytes back
> or they'll erase data, permanently in fact.

The kill switch accidentally detected
by a British man saved many in USA.
Upgrades by some, escaped being selected
from being hacked by tools from NSA.
> Shadow Brokers seek billions in a payday,
> benefitting from computers' heyday.

Hero frees from WannaCry ransomware,
but cyber-hackers will re-code.
It has become a digital nightmare.
We must be alert to what they upload.
> We do not know the crippling source
> of what has become a world-wide resource.

In 100 countries cyber-attacking
compromised companies, hospitals, universities.
Devastated data needs more backing
to prevent theft and health adversities.
> Computers help us communicate,
> calculate, create and innovate.

Cause of dangerous hacking
is bitcoin greed and sense of control?
Hackers are ransacking
our digital data and taking a tremendous toll
> on freedom of exchange,
> jeopardizing our future range.

Fearless Girl

"Fearless Girl" statue near Wall Street's *"Charging Bull"* statue

A defiant, 50-inch bronze statue–
      hands on hips, ponytail flailing
confronts the bull as a symbol of female
      empowerment and gender equality.

No glass ceiling for her–
      head high to the sky.
She's viral on social media. Celebrities,
      politicians, tourists take selfies with her.

Immovable, stalwart, her skirt lashes like a matador's cape.
      The 7000 pound bull bows his head to her.
Fearless Girl challenges companies to promote
      more women to their boards.

Some call her a publicity stunt. For others
      a reminder of cultural issues we need
to confront, a feminist marketing tool,
      a defamation of the longstanding bull.

Her publicity increased her sponsor's
      brand awareness and trading volume.
Fearless Girl is a global phenomenon–
      a part of society creating conversations.

Fearless Girl is part of a marketing trend
      touching on social issues to gain
good publicity and endear more customers.
      She's not buying any old bull.

A small statue of a urinating dog
      placed briefly beside her
was hauled away. No competition.
      Fearless Girl is a bull-fighter.

Pink Balloons
    Ariana Grande Concert, Manchester, England

Pink balloons rise to the ceiling
    at the end of the pop star concert.
        Elated girls and women's dreams and hopes
          empowered by music,
            their promise burst by a terrorist blast
              destroying their beliefs
                by someone who
                  does not believe in them.
Ariana Grande vows to return to Manchester.

Pro-Femina

On #MeToo women around the world
speak out against sexual harassment--
verbally and physically by abusive men.

Women have been indoctrinated, intimidated
dominated by men's desires, denied equal access
to education, jobs, opportunity, control over their body.

For too long men have viewed vaginas
as parking garages or holsters for their penises.
Their grabby hands violate, crush freedom, self-worth.

Increasing exposure of Bill Cosby, Donald Trump,
movie producers, priests and work place molestation--
silenced by threats and lawsuit settlements is overdue.

The evening news is full of protests against
inappropriate power use. Women need to feel safe
and empowered to confront and escape abuse.

After three decades as an editor reading
for a feminist journal, poetry and prose
by women attacked around the world--I am angry.

I am angry at all the stories of women's talents
diminished and lives stunted by demands of men--
the wasted lives because of men's disrespect and greed.

How many Malala's maimed? Yet she won the Nobel
Peace Prize and runs a foundation to educate girls
in places where they are denied access to education.

If women's roles around the world would open choices,
many women would not choose to give birth, do domestic tasks,
face poverty and men's wars, choose traditional roles, choose men.

I have been fortunate to have choices, chose a good mate,
chose education, chose children, chose my career.
But so many women don't have choices or are told they don't.

At the age of ten, three boys called my doll ugly.
I didn't like them insulting my doll and beat them
up-one at a time. One in front of his father.

I was finished with violent responses by high school.
A baton snatcher I whirled into a heap. A ponytail puller
on skates I twirled onto the ice to cool off.

In high school girls decided to wear skirts above the knees.
The principal confronted me in the hall to tell me my skirt
was too short. I said he wouldn't know if he weren't looking.

In college I remember frat boys trying to spike
my coke. I was vigilant and they did not succeed,
but I remember the women's stories who weren't.

I have heard my share of sexist jokes, crap rap,
listened to many molested women, read desperate
attempts women have taken to retrieve their lives.

I am angry at the sadness and pain after assault.
I recall outrunning a man to safety in college
as he chased me walking to the dorm.

I am angry the creators of life, art, science
have to live with the fear of male maleficence.
Time for an age of equality, respect and love.

I applaud Gloria Steinem, Oprah Winfrey,
feminists, Women's Marchers, all the suffragettes
the wall-crashers and glass ceiling breakers.

Fortunately the list is growing, breaking boundaries,
opening opportunities for women. Men may think
with their dicks, but women think with their brains.

With so many issues threatening our survival
we need the cooperation of everyone to solve them.
Obviously men need women's help cleaning up their mess.

I am angry I have to feel angry. I want to dream,
appreciate creativity and beauty everywhere in the cosmos.
Men are dropping their balls in every arena.

Time to pick up the games and let the gals play.
        Body autonomy. Brain strategies.
May all creatures find harmony and peace.

The Dirt on Men

Men never know when things are dirty or not. Emma by Jane Austen

Oh, I think men know
when things are dirty or not.
They wonder if the dirt will show.
They continue to muddy and plot.
 Will their dirt be caught?
 All their efforts are for naught?

When things are dirty or not,
men are accountable for their deeds.
Are they haves or have-nots?
They attempt their selfish needs.
 Some men treat others with respect.
 Some men exploit and neglect.

They wonder if their dirt will show.
Will their dastardly deeds be discovered?
Will dirty laundry foreshadow
many layers to be uncovered?
 Dirt minds, dirty hands
 these untouchables give commands.

They continue to muddy and plot
until victims take a stand
to redress the stain and ingrained spot,
display courage they don't understand.
 Overpowering others with evil–
 few want to sink to their level.

Will their dirt be caught,
sweep up, cleansed by laws?
They believe others can be bought,
pounce with predatory paws.
 Out, out damned spot, replace--
 expose them and bring disgrace.

All their efforts are for naught?
Will justice eventually prevail?
Well-intentioned men ought
to prevent perpetuating a dirty trail.
 Dirty old and young men act out
 leaving decency and morality in doubt.

#ResistMarch June 11, 2017

This year the LGBTQ community is lending its iconic rainbow flag to anyone
who feels their rights are under threat and to anyone who feels like America's
strength is diversity. Brian Pendelton

Tens of thousands of marchers resisting Trump policies
have closed the streets of L.A.. Many organizations
for Planned Parenthood, Climate Change, Obamacare.

Trump's star on the Hollywood Boulevard walk of fame
defamed with stickers: "I resist Homophobia" "I resist Transphobia"
"No! Drive out Trump/Pence Fascist Regime."

There is a Trump piñata with devil's horns.
Women wear pink capes and hats,
continuing resistance of Women's March.

A weekend of events ends with Democratic politician speakers:
Nancy Pelosi, Adam Schiff, Maxine Waters and actor Chris Rock.
Signs proclaim: "Love is love". "The world is better with love."

Cars cannot park on the parade route and lots of security.
Protest marches need to remain non-violent.
As long as there is injustice, we must march and resist.

In hundreds of marches and rallies thousands
remembered Pulse massacre in Orlando, fear Trump--
"We're here, we're queer, get that Cheeto out of here."

The Equality March in Washington was endorsed
by national advocacy groups concerned by Trump's
policies and anti-LBGT administration appointments.

The rainbow flag is a symbol to many groups
feeling discriminated against and disenfranchised.
"Love trumps hate" shout marchers for equality and justice.

Hateful Shadows

Trump–channeling and rallying those who still lend him their allegiance after his shameful response to what happened in Charlottesville–is something like a defiant lunar (possibly "lunatic") orb, stuck in place at full eclipse, defying even the laws of the universe and unwilling to budge.   Frank Fromherz

Tomorrow the solar eclipse's path of totality
leaves blue Oregon over mostly red states
who gave their electoral votes for Trump.

His stance has offended people of good will,
responsibility, opposition to hate and to perpetuating
the deplorable aspects of our nation's past.

Our past is HIStory, oppressing women,
Native Americans, Blacks, workers, exploiting
our nation's resources for greed, inequality.

Monuments to these ill-will baiters, traitors, should
be removed, put into a museum as a reminder
of what evil deeds wrought upon our people.

Trump is anti-science, anti-art, anti-intellectual,
anti-minorities, anti-women, anti-LBGTQ, anti-press,
anti-immigrant, anti-climate change, anti-environment...

anti-Muslim, anti-Semite, anti-diplomacy, anti-justice,
anti-good health care... – just a sexist, narcissistic, belligerent,
un-balanced, narrow-minded, under-educated predator.

Like the total eclipse, may the shadow of Trump
pass quickly back into the light and the nation's daymare
whether in the path of totality or not-- wake up and act.

Trump is "Sad"

If I'm to learn patience this incarnation,
I'm postponing patience until my next life experience.
I'm fed up with the Trump administration–
the destruction, obstruction, negligence,
      greed, attacks on education and science.
      They de-regulate, release compliance.

I'm postponing patience until my next life experience.
Trump is a world-wide embarrassment.
He's over his head in every situation, lacks intelligence.
Women and immigrants receive harassment.
      He's failed in domestic affairs and global summits.
      The world watches and ponders what he commits.

I'm fed up with the Trump administration–
the hacked election, he lost the popular vote.
They knee-jerk without diligent evaluation.
The USA's on a sinking boat, struggling to stay afloat.
      Unqualified appointments reverse progress--
      none achieve Obama's success.

The destruction, obstruction, negligence
disenfranchises millions for health care.
A climate changer denier, he reduces Earth's resilience.
The wall-builder seems uninformed and unaware.
      While he continues to fumble,
      our democracy begins to crumble.

Greed, attacks on education and science,
favors the rich and the one-percent.
We're isolated, without our reliance
on allies and refused Paris Accords consent.
      Education and the environment are under threat,
      and no equitable, sustainable health care yet.

They de-regulate, free compliance
as coal pollutes water, oil fracks land.
Banks freed for fraud, trust up to chance.
I refuse to accept or understand.
      He attacks free press and free speech.
      When will Congress take action to impeach?

Another Bloody Mess

The president's tweets today don't help our political or national discourse and do
not provide a positive role for our nation's dialogue.
Rep. James Lankford, Oklahoma

The day after another Trump tweet bloody mess,
calling Morning Joe co-hosts "crazy" and "psycho",
and accused the woman of low I.Q. and a bloody facelift.

I sit in the sun after a blood draw–bandages on right hand
and left elbow crease. Not in the mood for blood-letting
or another outrageous outburst from the Tweet Twit.

How many women will he attack with tiny hands,
contempt, inappropriate conduct and words?
He's wants to take women's health care as well.

Trump's indelicate, sexist, disrespectful, erroneous tweet
is considered undignified for the office-- a rare bipartisan
agreement on the uncivil, anti-women, wall and ban builder.

The tweets united Democrats and Republicans
in a chorus of protest for his abnormal behavior,
the loudest outcry so far. Is he out of his mind?

Health care, immigration, education, environment,
ill-advised appointments, divisive cabinet, the epitome
of greed, injustice, negative "isms", boastful incompetence.

Melania is starting a campaign against bullying.
She might start at home. He is the child with small hands
grasping for Cheerios, like mini-life rafts.

This immature, misguided stunted child, consults
with world leaders who ridicule him. He shouldn't
represent us with such low approval and sense.

I tug off the beige elasticized wraps and cotton balls,
just a small dot of blood. My heart bleeds more.
I feel I could gush an arterial volcano.

216

Trumpifiring

Translated from Swedish Trumpifiering: Trumpifiring is a word related to populism, and is based on Donald Trump's rhetorical style during his presidential election in 2016. The word was coined by opponents of Donald Trump and points to positions such as popular beliefs are the true views. The word includes invented news, lies, insults and denials of previous statements. (1) Language Council and Language Newsletter defines the word as "changing the political debate toward a rhetorical style where one says that receives attention without taking into account consistency or facts." Wikipedia

My Swedish relative who sent "The Golden Toupee"
sent "trumpifiering" to me today.
We had to translate from Swedish to English.
My guesses-- not as close as I'd wish.

I thought pilfer, interfering or firing,
but not the detail I was desiring.
When its meaning became clear,
it clutched heart and mind in fear.

Trumps distortions, uninformed decisions, lies...
By his tweets, cronies, executive orders he tries
to bully the nation, take away what majority wants.
Unaccountable, when confronted, he rants.

There is something wrong with a system when
more voted against him. It's like Gore again.
He's destroying health care, environment, all
to puff rich pockets, military, build unnecessary wall.

It does not seem he gets any issue right,
ignores the poor, the immigrants' plight.
Even the Republican Congress pondering reelection,
might wonder if they should support Trump's selection.

His staff, appointees and he's under investigation
for Russian ties, hacking, rigging the election allegation.
Every day his policy damages, rampages
attacking, fracking the treasures of past ages.

He's uninformed domestically and globally also.
The time has come–he has to go.
We are overwhelmed by his detritus.
Unite! Trump won't stand beside us.

Swollen Minds

Where little minds belong to rich people in authority, they have a knack of swelling out till they are quite as unmanageable as great ones. Emma by Jane Austen

Trump is not the only rich,
white, privileged, man kind
who lusts to exploit others.
CEOs and sexual predators come to mind.

Their power plays, betraying trust,
take unfair advantage.
Now people are speaking out,
rebelling in outrage.

Trump is the symbol of little minds
with tiny hands and brief tweets.
He stands for bullying, bluster,
mentally unbalanced deceits.

In these perilous times Trump leads
world to a dangerous edge.
His trigger finger, itchy for a fight.
He must not fulfill his pledge.

Someday the 99% will rise
to claim share from 1% top.
Such injustice and greed are reprehensible.
Someday such inequity must stop.

Trump is in "Adult Day Care",
but with unreliable supervision.
He displays his global ignorance
and thrives on fear and division.

Trump has not been held accountable
for his disgusting and immoral actions.
Investigations could reveal illegitimate election
collusion, illegal real estate and tax transactions.

Trump embarrasses most of our nation,
the butt of jokes around the world.
He's a pumpkin head without light.
Will dark jack-o-lantern be hurled?

Alaskan Haiku

Drunk trees toppled
in tundra as permafrost melts
methane sighs to sky

Alaskan Native Americans
witness ocean nibbling villages
losing way of life

try wind and solar power
we cannot sustain oil and gas
need for coal declines

wildlife domain diminished
dwell beside oil equipment
no deal with pipelines

carbon increases warms
climate change caused by us
threatens survival

roadways buckle highway
heave earth beneath losing grip
lids on nature erupt

Consider seven generations
we are running out of time
to turn the tide protect the earth.

Whacks for July 4th Holiday 2017

Whacks from the Election: Headlines suggest we "fire up the 4th."
My enthusiasm muted by bombardments on our liberty,
treasured values by incompetent leadership, bully puppet.
It seems fewer flags are flown. Fewer patriotic costumes flaunted.

Whacks from a Baseball Game: The evening of July 3rd a sell-out crowd
watched Corvallis Knights defeat Bend Elks 8-1 on balmy clear night.
Throwing, frozen t-shirt contests, followed by spectacular fireworks.
I'm red (blanket), white (ghostly white skin) and blue hoodie.

Whacks to Tiny Valley Towns: My husband, grandson and I did not march in local
All-American, Anyone Can Join, Fabulous, Fantastic Fourth of July parade.
We drove north toward the sea with fuzzy destinations.

We drove through tiny, former farming and timber towns.
Old houses, vacant store fronts, family grocery stores, reviving
with cannabis emporiums, wine and gift shops, small restaurants.

Whacks to Seaside Towns: We wove through back roads going and coming,
into the mire of tourist traps, lodging, in and out of tsunami hazard zones.
I hope when a big one comes we have flying cars. Evacuation routes clog.

Whacks to Diet: We were not sure what will be open on the fourth. Fast food yes.
Many restaurants no. We settled for a well-known chain. Relatively
clean and healthy. Kind people of all races hold doors for each other.

Whacks on Metal: Over the long, high Megler bridge into Washington.
Coast is mostly undeveloped with small towns like Raymond
with magnificent, rusted, thin metal sculptures of animals and people.

Whacks at Forests: Moth-eaten mountains. Stumps, stubble, clear cuts--
various stages of re-planting. Gouged earth, root balls. Wildflowers
edge the whacking with lupine, Queen Anne's lace, daisies, yellow dots.

Whacks at Rap: Part of our grandson's Smart Phone musical repertoire
is what I call crap rap- narcissistic, sexist, demeaning men whining,
moaning, lusty lyrics which heavy beats mostly drown out—gratefully.

Whacks at Aberdeen: We head for a park with a memorial to Kurt Cobain.
The town museum was closed, but they have a walking tour
for their famous, Grunge musician, local boy. The bridge where he wrote.

Grandson wanted to see the cement guitar on a pedestal, two metal
facial images and two sided sign. Much less impressive
than Jimi Hendrick's mini-temple in Seattle and Cobain's death home.

I wore my black Nirvana with white angel t-shirt I bought
in Seattle with grandson. In my sunglasses I pose
beside the lackluster, gray guitar and chipped black base.

A mural on Wishwah Street commemorates several bands–
Nirvana, Foo Fighters, Mud Honey, Sound Garden, Pearl Jam,
Alice in Chains, Temple of the Dog, Candlebox and others,
on a colorful band like a glistening wrestler's belt. Very eye-catching.

Aberdeen has several murals. One has flags of the early immigrants.
Cobain's house is on the route. His music store closed. We cross Wishwah
bridge, listen to " Something in the Way" where his ashes washed away.

*Underneath the bridge/ the tarp has sprung a leak.. And I'm living off of grass
and the drippings from the ceiling...Something in the way ah ahh* Partial lyrics
on a sign. Under the bridge graffiti of song titles and his portrait.

Whacks at Astoria: The white caps of the waves, Victorian homes, lure us
back many times. The museums are closed. Did not see trolley.
Goonie house forbidden to drive or walk to-or photograph now.

The restored Astoria tower recorded Astoria's past, soars
to a spectacular vista. The guys climbed to the top. As I gazed
over slightly hazy landscape toward the sea from the parking lot.

Mo's just opened a seafood, seafront restaurant. Through wide windows
pilot boats lead ships over the bar, seagulls perched on jagged posts.
Delicious clam chowder attacks my taste buds and garlic cheese bread.

Whacks of Wildlife: Leaving Astoria three deer munch school yard grass,
rural home hosts two deer on their lawn, one deer crosses road.
Several elk viewing places revealed no elk.

Whacks on Back Roads: In one place washed out road was gravel, guys
switch driving and musical selections. Sitka spruce stumps left
from use in building war planes. Sunset laces shadows.

Whacks of Fireworks: From 9:45-10:30 as we drove down the valley,
fireworks spark-speckled the sky on both side of the roads.
We watched big crowds for small towns gatherings for their fireworks.

It was fascinating to watch above treetops and between buildings,
light displays pop out unexpectedly and various distances. Fireworks
firing up the fourth with blasts, pops, cascades in light-altered sky.

Spots of light and hope in our nation's whacky darkness.
Independence from destruction and violence toward liberty
for the people, environment, health care, education etc.

By 11:30 we were home and learn North Korea's whacked
dictator is ballistic with missiles. Unpredictable, impulsive
Trump could lead us into another war for our independence.

Derailed

When the Seattle train derailed over I-5
on its initial commuter run, causing
casualties and deaths, it was symbolic
of the entire derailed 2017 reality.

Ever since the Trump administration
reduced regulations, environmental protections,
health care services, educational reforms,
dreamers and immigrants futures–derailed.

Sexual harassment, women's empowerment,
accountability, male privilege challenged,
sometimes Trump's agenda provokes
people to step up and take action.

His disregard for our citizens, global
responsibilities, endangering peace,
taxes favoring rich, irresponsible tweets,
outright lies, collusion–a sexual predator...

He clouded the world in 2017. Can we weather
the storm or will climate change, war,
stupidity lead to our extinction. We hope
for relief from these deluded off-rail people.

Do we have time for the investigators
to arrest these greedy, dangerous-- mostly men?
January will bring more marches, lawsuits.
We are off track– cars linked to an out-of-control engine.

We must take back our power. Fuel a positive engine.
Get back on a progressive schedule. Repair old tracks.
Lay new ones. We cannot afford more delays.
Can we get on track before it is too late?

Searching for Truths

You must stand up to truth about it, speak about it, and light up the Earth with your power, love, and kindness. Linda and Terry Jamison

Each morning I click on the Bing icon
    to see the beautiful screen image,
site filled with fantastic photos
    from around the world and cosmos.

Beneath is a string of slides
    telling of global and celestial events
which you can pick and click on
    to learn more details.

Today KKK founder statue painted pink,
    Star RZ Piscium is eating its planets,
e-waste recycled into art in Africa, NASA
    plans to go to Alpha Centuri in 2069.

There is the political news,
    the entertainment gossip,
celebrity deaths, crimes, taxes,
    quirky events of hope ...or not.

We have to beware of hacking,
    fake news, persist and resist
for truths–speak out, march,
    light candles of hope.

I am glad I have the choice
    to go in more depth on Bing topics
I am curious about and reject
    the negative events engulfing us.

On any screens we have options
    that can enhance our attitude
promote love and kindness.
    We can use our power and light wisely.

In person to person contacts
    we need to be selective
and surround ourselves
    with up-vibe people when we can.

Some days all this is very hard.

First Supermoon This Year

It is January 1st 2018
A Supermoon makes the scene.
Put on shoes and go outside.
Watch light and dark collide.

Starting the year with light close
is hopeful for 2017 was morose.
Predictions for this year contradict,
so not sure what cosmos will inflict.

But starting year with a Supermoon
I will forgo casting cards or rune
and stop looking at prophecy sites
to perceive bright omens in nights.

What will come, I can't foresee
but a Supermoon will dazzle me.
For a moment I will release sorrow,
leave persist and resist for tomorrow.

Lacunae of Light

We live in everyone. I live in you.
You live in me. There is no gap, no distance.

Amit Ray

Bridging the Gaps

There are gaps in understanding and point of view.
There are gaps in knowledge so far unknown.
There are gaps in relationships hard to undo.
There are gaps we won't fill and call our own.
    Which gaps will we try to bridge?
    Which gaps are our privilege?

There are gaps in knowledge so far unknown
in fossil records and past civilizations.
Theories how life on Earth has grown
and the entity or committee for these creations.
    Panspermia, starseeds, DNA codes?
    So many contexts where life explodes.

There are gaps in relationships hard to undo
when there are gaps in kindness and logic.
There is just so much intervention can do
when things get violent and toxic.
    When is the best time to try or let go?
    Gaps can be wide and deep to hoe.

There are gaps we won't fill and call our own
because heart and mind will not go there.
Gaps can crack the cornerstone
of our basic core values of where
    we would prefer not to fill gaps with rubble
    or deflate our integrity's bubble.

Which gaps will we try to bridge?
Personal, national, global concerns?
Will my impact help to abridge
to a peaceful situation my heart yearns?
    When do I know I have overcome my stay
    and have the courage to walk away?

Which gaps are our privilege
to have the opportunity to make a difference?
Do we want to prevent a sacrilege?
Do we have the guts to confront offense?
    So much injustice and cruel pain.
    Fill gaps for an even plane?

Filling Gaps With Light

My masseuse checks my chakras
for darkness, pulls out black cords
and threads with help of my angels
and fills chakras with golden light.

In the cosmos, the vast void
is filled with sparks of light.
Stars sparkle to enlighten
our darkled world.

Kindness and compassion,
rescue by strangers makes
some good news in the bleak news,
keeps hope alive.

Dreaming, laughing, creating,
watching works of art and science
reveal beauty and wonder,
lights an internal wick to glow.

When I leave my massage
I am lightened. Head clouds disappear.
I am balanced, warm-stoned, stretched,
moistened, ready to bring light.

Sources of Light

round sun tunnel
penetrates boundaries
wormholes light.

Rectangular skylight
like mirror
reflects light

dormant lamp
seeks darkness
to turn-on shine

illuminate clocks, microwaves
cells, electronic gear
communicate glow

flashlight beams
amid shadows
finding what's hidden

computer screen
captures images
with electronic light

flat like a mini-flashlight
spotlighting a doll collection
on stage on shelves

television receives
light and sound
by airwaves

follow street-lights
and lamp-posts
to travel in the dark

avoid dark lightning
during thunderstorms
and less lethal lightning

starlight in dark matter
sparkles what darkles
in our universe

inspiration
brightens minds
to enlighten world

follow gateways and portals
to other dimensions
to bring back light

twist time and light
spin neutrons into binary codes
travel to bring wormholes.

If Life is But a Dream

All that we see or seem is but a dream within a dream. Edgar Allan Poe

If
life
is but
dreaming in
series of dreams in
multiple dimensions, perhaps

we
have
past lives
after-lives
several current
lives dreaming in many places.

Are
we
living
just this–now
consciousness, wiping
clean other slates, writing record?

What
dreams
come true
somewhere some
time to multiple,
timeless mes when I do wake up?

Children of the Earth Monument

For Universal Children's Day, Bing featured a photo
of the Children of the Earth Monument in North Cape,
Norway glistening in sun, embedded in snow
like chocolate frosting on top of chocolate cookies.

The monument consists of seven bronze disks
encased in granite made by seven children from
Tanzania, Brazil, USA, Japan, Thailand, Italy, Russia
on clay tablets enlarged and bronzed in 1989.

The children ages 8-12 stayed in a nearby fishing
settlement for a week expressing their creativity
and emotions on clay tablets for friendship, hope,
joy and working together harmoniously.

The images were of an African man, self-portrait,
beast from the past, bird of peace, image of Christ,
a lady with a bow in rain and sunshine and a man
with a beard the artist wanted to be a cat.

A bronze sculpture Mother and Child by Eva Rybaken
shows a boy beside his mother pointing at the disks.
Together they form the Children of the Earth Monument.
In the background is a Globe Monument.

North Cape Hall is at the site with a theater,
restaurant, snack bar and post office,
an underground gallery and grotto with
a concert hall, bar and gift shop.

The Children of Earth Prize is given here yearly
to the individual or project showing compassion
and help for suffering children around the world.
The prize is about $18,000 US dollars.

Many see the monument perched on a high cliff
from a cruise ship. Cars face a steep climb up often
foggy, narrow, twisting road to the top to view this
expression of youthful understanding, cooperation, joy.

Start Each Day
   Start each day with a positive thought and a grateful heart. Roy T. Bennett

Start each day with positive thoughts and gratitude,
an uplifting intention.
Start each day with hope and upbeat attitude.
Pay attention.
   Start each day in the flow.
   Start each day in the know.

An uplifting intention
lets you rise up to confront challenges.
Negative retention
which positivity avenges
   might be chased out the door
   unlocking and freeing you once more.

Start each day with hope and upbeat attitude.
Clear the clouds, deal with the pain.
This all might sound like a platitude
but we can't let negativity reign.
   It can be hard to get up some days
   to find some aspects of life to praise.

Pay attention
to your inner and outer conditions.
I can mention
you create your life script, select renditions.
   We can't guarantee control or free will.
   You can at least try to act it still.

Start each day in the flow.
Some say align with cosmic energy.
See where your intuition can go.
Discover synchronicity and synergy.
   Share your gifts, heart and mind.
   Be compassionate and kind.

Start each day in the know
expecting the best despite what you discover.
Think it will turn around, can shine away shadow.
It is time for Gaia and good folks to take over.
   Perform the mission you were sent here!
   Bring light and overcome fear.

Walk-Kissers

Walk as if you are kissing the Earth with your feet. Thich Nhat Hanh

Probably more kissing foot to ground if barefoot,
but smelly feet suck-facing Earth idea
might have lead to inventing shoes.

This kissing-up to Earth could be gratitude
for grounding and protection from rough spots--,
affection and appreciation for beauty.

When I walk I often have my walker
adding more contact points to draw chi
from Gaia and cosmos. Prevents falling.

I look where I walk, pay attention.
My feet long to dance and tread
more lightly on the surface.

Flapping feet on groomed ground
for sports, fans standing and shouting
are in their way kissing Earth.

Most often I am dealing with floors,
a separation from direct contact.
Layers of coverings prevent foot-Earth-kissing.

Aging ailments prevent going barefoot.
Shoes touch grass. I press my sole
to connect to life's energy with a smooch.

Or I can romp in my wheelchair
throwing kisses to all the dwellers
who walk on this Earth.

Light Showers

At 5:00 pm. The timer splayed
sparks of red and green
through the uncurtained window
darting across the ceiling
from the light shower gizmo
in the front yard.

Lines of light parading
in and out, performing patterns.
My own panspermia of life-light,
contingent of mini-comets,
all festive for the festivals of light.
They are like genetically altered
pollywogs-- DNA tweaked to glow,
swimming on my emblazoned ceiling.

A battalion of blazing mini-tennis balls
back and forth over an invisible net?
Whatever fantasy I imagine
somehow I do not want
to close the curtain and step
outside to see the light-splattered
front wall of the house.
It is too cold.

Reluctantly I close the curtain
and to my delight through the thin veil
a swarm of luminous lightning bugs dance
in fervent frenzy until at midnight
the timer blinks them out.

However, the timer on the new wreath
with a ring of lighted angels looped
on the doorknob on the other side
of the blue-shaded french doors
was miss-set and over my head
in my bed I had a halo of light
until 3 in the morning.

To Be or Not To Be

For me, when I say spiritual, I'm referring to a feeling you would have that connects you to the universe in a way that defies simple vocabulary. We think about the universe as an intellectual playground, which it surely is, but the moment you learn something that touches an emotion rather than just something intellectual, I would call that a spiritual encounter with the universe. Neil deGrasse Tyson

To be or not to be is not my question
because we seem to be, but not know how
we came to be, hence my suggestion
we choose our own explanation somehow.
    Belief in intelligent design?
    Science does not always align.

Because we seem to be, but not know how
the multiverse and consciousness started,
we find some theory and kowtow
or try some ideas and then departed.
    My spirituality does not have a name.
    Agnostic is the closest claim.

We came to be, hence my suggestion
we remain open and curious for answers.
Ah, such phenomenally, complex reflection!
We are part of frabjous cosmic dancers.
    Some Omni-sparkler lit the spark
    to bring light and also created dark.

We choose our own explanation somehow
from ingrained religious or other areas of thought.
Some choices are restricted. Some cultures don't allow
freedom of exploration, words wisdom thinkers brought.
    I've ridden on a spiritual merry-go-round.
    I've reached for the ring–still not found.

Belief in intelligent design
amid observed chaos and violence
brings hope someone's in charge--divine--
will resolve disorder, pain and silence
    all the anxiety to promote peace.
    All disturbances could release.

Science does not always align
with an utopian surreality.
Many are still looking for a sign
to comprehend this perceived reality.
    To be or not to be seems out of our comprehension.
    For now I'll keep all my commitments in suspension.

The Character Gap

Our hearts are not morally pure, but they are not morally corrupt either.
Rather, they are a messy blend of good and evil. Christian Miller

Philosophers ponder if we are pure of heart
or rotten to the core. Mencius for benevolence
while Confucian Xunzi for our nature is bad.
Angels and devils may be extremes
when balance gets out of whack?

Does our behavior depend on context
of opportunity to act well or badly?
Our surroundings influence us but
we are very inconsistent? Are most
of us somewhere on the spectrum?

We are rarely fully virtuous or vicious?
Character is a consistent set of traits?
Good or bad actions lead to appropriate
or wrong reasoning? Vices can lead
to bad actions? Who is judging?

Most people bounce around in context
have no virtues or vices? Context
of actions hard to test to indicate character?
Miller's research leaves questions and
perplexing conundrums.

He suggests we are more likely to help
someone if we are reminded of bad things
we have done in the past or if we believe
people will notice our selfishness? But some
say guilt and embarrassment are relief not virtue.

Some strategies to fill in gaps include
using nudges, wait for age and experience
to improve us, reinforce good behavior
with virtue words–but concludes not workable.
Good role models don't build good character.

He suggests religious approach to building
character. Reason and science give way to faith.
Research does not back this up. A study
indicated religious upbringings lead to less
altruistic people. Many moral gaps unfilled.

Theorists debate about following moral laws
or judging each case on its merits. Some
debate difference between altruism and virtue.
Agree in harmony between flourishing of individual
and the good of others over extreme self-sacrifice.

Miller believes character is built, not given.
His research is biased toward Christian values.
Other moral philosophers look at a more worldly
viewpoint. Pick your perspective. Develop your slant
on your character from your preferred resources.

Character is relative. Practices performed
in previous times are not PC today. We try
to change "isms" that exclude, decrease
injustice and inequality. Filling the gaps
with such differences of opinion is hard.

Many issues have strong proponents
of their point of view which they consider
virtuous and others perceive as evil. Cultures
find cramps on freedom and progress
as a continuing problem and frustration.

Several extremist cults and groups
feeling they are bettering the world
do not sit well with those of opposing views.
We are in a dualistic reality. Light/dark.
Will we ever get the gaps fulfilled—enlightened?

Time's Up

We no longer live in the blank white spaces at the edge of print. We no longer live in the gaps between the stories. We are the stories in print and we are writing the stories ourselves. Elizabeth Moss

Women are speaking up, being believed and heard.
Sexual misconduct, intimidation, inequity displayed.
Women are empowered by their word.
Women no longer will be betrayed.
>Men of good character stand by her side.
>Women will take command of their lives with pride.

Sexual misconduct, intimidation, inequity displayed
will no longer be tolerated by women globally.
Women's talents and dreams dismissed, delayed
because overpowering men acted ignobly.
>Uniting for an empowered future,
>women have themselves to nurture.

Women are empowered by their word.
to take legal action, prevent gender inequalities.
Women have generations to gird,
cultural values to change and create new realities
>for women world-wide who are oppressed
>and their viewpoints not expressed.

Women no longer will be betrayed
by enablers, men who exploit their power.
Men should be ashamed of the roles they played.
They could not have stooped lower
>than to limit women's freedom, truth and disrespect
>their rights of choice and their due respect.

Men of good character stand by her side,
promote equal opportunities and access,
support strong women with confident stride
and celebrate their success.
>All must work together to solve problems
>not divided by cultural restraints or anthems.

Women will take command of their lives with pride
not impeded by greedy grabs by men.
Everyone is to join in for the hopeful ride
for an enhanced future when all are freed again,
    for time is up for old ways of seeing.
    There is a new way for all of being.

For too long women have not been heard or believed if they dared to speak their power to those men. But their time is up. Their time is up. A new day is on the horizon. Oprah Winfrey

Acknowledgments
Filling the Gaps in Publications

- Poetry Books -
Cinqueries: A Cluster of Cinquos and Lanternes
Fibs and Other Truths
Black Stars on a White Sky
Poems That Count
Poems That Count Too
*Winging-It: New And Selected Poems
*Red Cape Capers: Playful Backyard Meditations
*Star Stuff: A Soul-Splinter Experiences the Cosmos
*Light-Headed: A Soul-Splinter Experiences Light
*Sparks: A Soul-Splinter Experiences Earth
*Into the Clouds: Seeking Silver Linings
*Mirabilia: Manifesting Marvels, Miracles and Mysteries
*Spiral Hands: Signs for Healing

* Lulu.com/spotlight/rainbowcom/

- Chapbooks -
Being Cosmic, Intra-Space Chronicles
Light-Headed, Red Cape Capers

- On-Line Web-site Books on Forms -
Free access: @ www.rainbowcommunications.org
Syllables of Velvet
Word-Playful
Poetluck

- Anthologies -
The Second Genesis
Branches
Poetic License
Poetic License 2015
Jubilee
The Eloquent Umbrella

Twelve Novels in the Rainbow Chronicle Series.

www.ingramcontent.com/pod-product-compliance
Lightning Source LLC
Chambersburg PA
CBHW031832090426
42741CB00005B/210